MASTERING THE MODERN DATA STACK

An Executive Guide to Unified Business Analytics

Nick Jewell, Ph.D.

It's not the tech that's tiny, just the book![TM]

TinyTechMedia LLC

Mastering the Modern Data Stack:
An Executive Guide to Unified Business Analytics

by Nick Jewell, Ph.D.

Published By:

TinyTechMedia LLC

Editor: Peter Letzelter-Smith
Cover Designer: Josipa Ćaran Šafradin
Proofreader / Indexer: Peter Letzelter-Smith
Typesetter / Layout: Ravi Ramgati
September 2023: First Edition
Revision History for the First Edition
2023-09-28: First Release
ISBN: (paperback) : 979-8-9858227-6-2
ISBN: (eBook) : 979-8-9858227-8-6

www.TinyTechGuides.com

In Praise Of

David Matyáš, Principal Analytics Consultant

"Nick Jewell did an awesome job in consolidating the knowledge built over the last decade of modern data architectures into a guide that you inhale in an hour, saving tons of time. Incredible!"

Scott Brown, Distinguished Engineer, Financial Services

"Comprehensive, concise, and actionable—a highly readable resource for anyone trying to wrangle the modern data challenge in their business! Nick's TinyTechGuide helps you find a clear path through the complex and challenging world of the modern data landscape."

Shaan Mistry, Data Innovator

"If you're truly curious about modern data architecture, this is a must-read! Finally, a book that demystifies the Modern Data Stack without getting caught up in vendor or VC hype!"

Dedication

"For Kirsteen, Lottie, and Joe"

"The only reason to move or integrate data is to monetize it."

Generally Agreed-Upon Information Principle #17[1]
Jonathan Wray, Co-Founder, Aible
2023 CDOIQ Symposium

Prologue

TinyTechGuides are designed for practitioners, business leaders, and executives who never seem to have enough time to learn about the latest technology and trends. These guides are designed to be read in an hour or two and focus on applying technologies in a business, government, or educational setting.

After reading this guide, I hope you'll better understand the diverse range of capabilities of the Modern Data Stack. This includes how it is applied in the real world and how to make informed decisions around future data architecture strategy and best practices for unified business analytics in your business or organization.

Wherever possible, I share practical advice and lessons learned during my career so you can transform this hard-won knowledge into action.

Remember, it's not the tech that's tiny, just the book!™

If you're interested in writing a TinyTechGuide, please visit www.TinyTechGuides.com

Conventions Used

There are several text conventions used throughout this book, which focuses on exploring Modern Data Stack functionality and potential. One of them is highlighting vendors deemed significant to specific capabilities. A name in **bold** indicates the first mention of a vendor. Subsequent mentions will not be in bold format.

Here is an example: "While cloud-based data warehousing was gaining momentum, another significant development was taking place: the rise of **Apache Spark**."

Tips or important notes
Appear like this.

Contents

CHAPTER 3

CHAPTER 4

CHAPTER 5

CHAPTER 7

CHAPTER 8

CHAPTER 1

Introduction

The Need for the Modern Data Stack

In today's era of digital transformation, the effective capture, management, and use of data sits atop business agendas. The growing volumes of data, and executive-level demands to make faster and smarter decisions using data, analytics, automation, and artificial intelligence (AI) mean that organizations find traditional data management systems, infrastructure, and architectures inadequate.

This is where the concept of the Modern Data Stack steps in.

The Modern Data Stack is a collection of tools, cloud-data technologies, and methodologies used to collect, process, store, and analyze data at scale.

The Modern Data Stack is far more than just a fad dreamt up by vendor marketing teams. It's a proven, "battle-tested," and flexible architecture that enables more efficient and effective data management, which ultimately delivers better business outcomes.[2] The stack provides the foundation for digital transformation that aids in the simplification or remediation of legacy solutions and the use of data-driven insights in broader business strategy.

Data leaders should consider adopting a Modern Data Stack to transform their organization's data capabilities, which will lead to better decision-making, increased efficiency, and competitive advantage.

Describing the Modern Data Stack

At the highest level, a data stack is defined as consisting of five core functional areas:

Figure 1.1: High-Level Functional Architecture of the Modern Data Stack

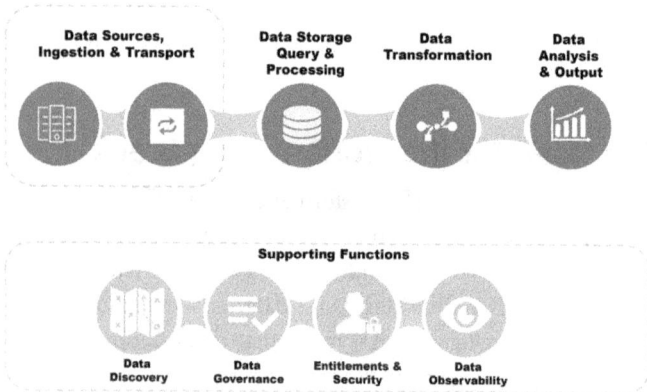

- **Data Sources, Ingestion, and Transport**: Where the data originates and how it's moved to the stack (see Chapter 3).
- **Data Storage, Query, and Processing**: Managing the data within the stack (see Chapter 4).
- **Data Transformation**: Reshaping the data to answer specific queries and build consistency in data definitions for analytics (see Chapter 5).
- **Data Analysis and Output**: Extracting value from the data in various forms (see Chapter 6).
- **Supporting Functions**: Making sure everything operates smoothly and with strong governance (see Chapter 7).

Depending on the project, organization, and long-term strategy, the goal will be to develop and implement these five functional areas in incremental phases, adjusting and fine-tuning components to meet the needs of stakeholders.

The following chapters will dive into each functional area, highlighting key components, challenges, and considerations for building a successful modern data strategy based on various scenarios and environments.

The Benefits of the Modern Data Stack

Figure 1.2: Benefits of the Modern Data Stack

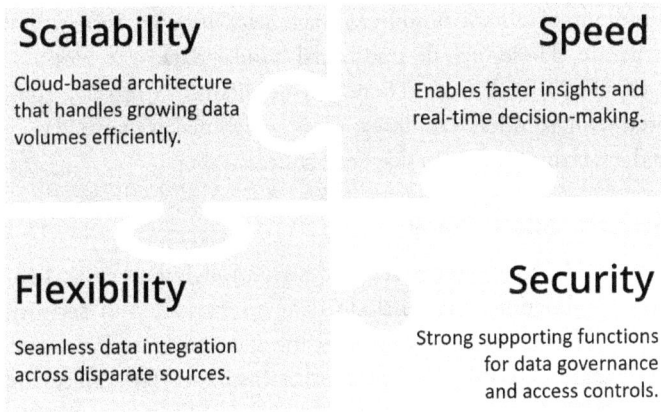

Scalability

Cloud-based architecture that handles growing data volumes efficiently.

Speed

Enables faster insights and real-time decision-making.

Flexibility

Seamless data integration across disparate sources.

Security

Strong supporting functions for data governance and access controls.

Innovative companies are adopting the Modern Data Stack for many compelling reasons, including:

Scalability

The ability to create scalable data architectures is critical in the current data landscape. Traditional systems often struggle with large data volumes, making it hard to scale up as an organization grows. In contrast, modern data architectures typically include cloud-based solutions that can quickly expand to handle increasing data loads. This means that a system can grow with an organization, providing consistent performance regardless of data volumes or the number of users.

Speed

The speed of processing and analysis directly impacts a firm's ability to compete effectively. A Modern Data Stack processes vast quantities of data quickly, enabling quicker insights and real-time decision-making, all of which allow organizations to be more agile and responsive to shifting business conditions.

Flexible Data Integration

The Modern Data Stack brings significant flexibility to data integration challenges. Organizations today often have data from hundreds of potential sources, each with its own format and structure. These include traditional tabular data, text files, images, videos, and more. There will be discussion of stack tools producing seamless data integration, which makes consolidating and analyzing data from disparate sources easier.

Security and Privacy

Good architecture and systems design strongly emphasize supporting functions that include data governance and security. With privacy regulations such as the General Data Protection Regulation (GDPR) and the Health Insurance Portability and Accountability Act (HIPAA) putting solid obligations regarding the data processing of personal information, it's crucial to have robust systems in place to protect sensitive data and ensure compliance. Modern Data Stack tools are designed for these needs, providing advanced security measures, privacy controls, and governance capabilities.

Do I Need All of This Functionality?

Let's be honest, it's *doubtful* that you'll need to implement every aspect of the Modern Data Stack to deliver significant value to your business. At least, not on day one. Not even in *year one*.

The purpose of this book isn't to sell a series of expensive "check boxes" in a project plan that will somehow guarantee successful delivery and stakeholder satisfaction. Instead, elaborating on

Figure 1.3: A Deeper Dive into the Modern Data Stack

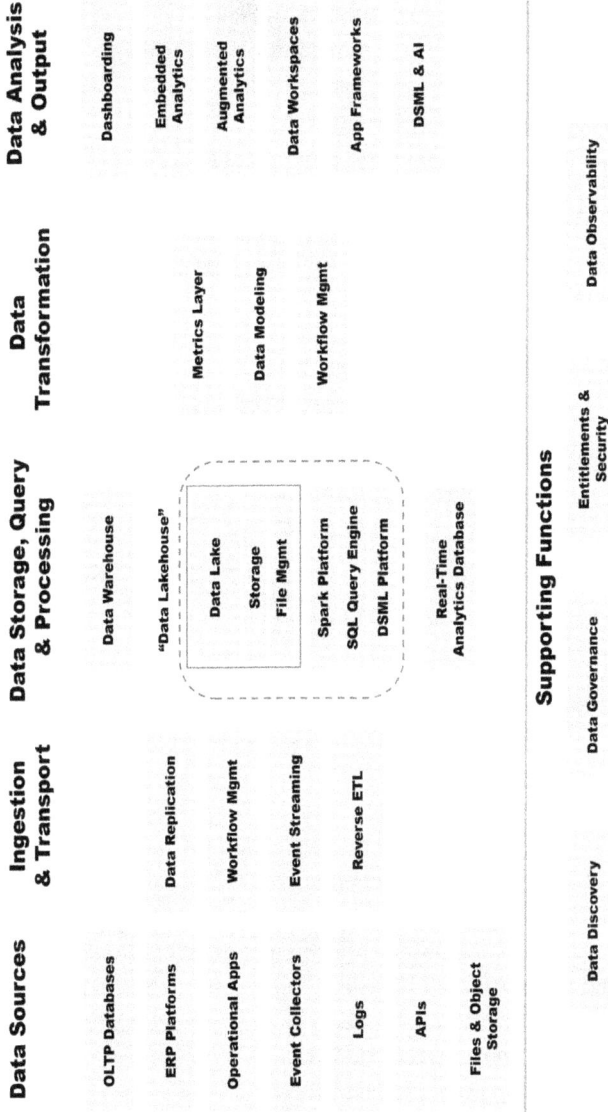

functional architecture from earlier, a series of building blocks that cover almost every imaginable data and analytics scenario will be touched upon, as shown in Figure 1.3.

Let's say that a small or medium-sized business with a modest range of data sources is looking to drive better decisions through the use of data. Exploring how cloud-based data warehousing and primary data pipelines can feed into dashboards or embedded analytics is a good way to get started.

The first steps with the Modern Data Stack might only require activating a few such building blocks to deliver real value, as shown in Figure 1.4.

Figure 1.4: Activating Initial Components of the Modern Data Stack for a Small/Mid-Sized Organization

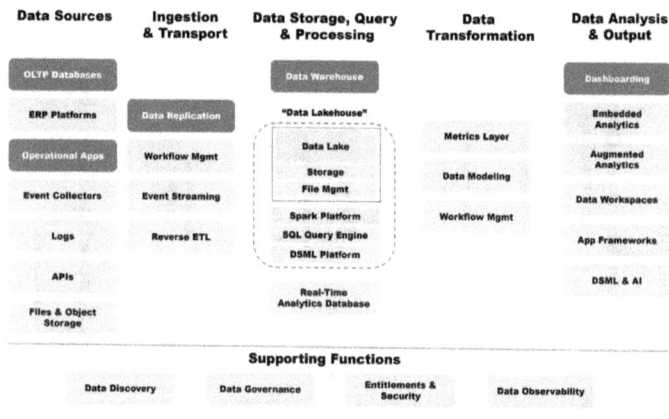

Data Sources	Ingestion & Transport	Data Storage, Query & Processing	Data Transformation	Data Analysis & Output
OLTP Databases		Data Warehouse		Dashboarding
ERP Platforms	Data Replication	"Data Lakehouse"		Embedded Analytics
Operational Apps	Workflow Mgmt	Data Lake	Metrics Layer	Augmented Analytics
Event Collectors	Event Streaming	Storage / File Mgmt	Data Modeling	Data Workspaces
Logs	Reverse ETL	Spark Platform / SQL Query Engine	Workflow Mgmt	App Frameworks
APIs		DSML Platform		DSML & AI
Files & Object Storage		Real-Time Analytics Database		

Supporting Functions

Data Discovery	Data Governance	Entitlements & Security	Data Observability

In a larger, more complex enterprise environment, there may be many more diverse data sources to ingest and transform in delivering analytical outcomes. As analytical maturity and sophistication grow, there's often a growing appetite for data environments (such as the data lakehouse) that cater to the mixed workloads of data scientists and AI engineers and the need for better data governance and workflow management practices.

Our first Modern Data Stack architecture for the enterprise, shown in Figure 1.5, takes on considerably more functionality (and complexity) to meet these goals.

Figure 1.5: Contrasting the Initial Components of the Modern Data Stack for Larger Enterprises

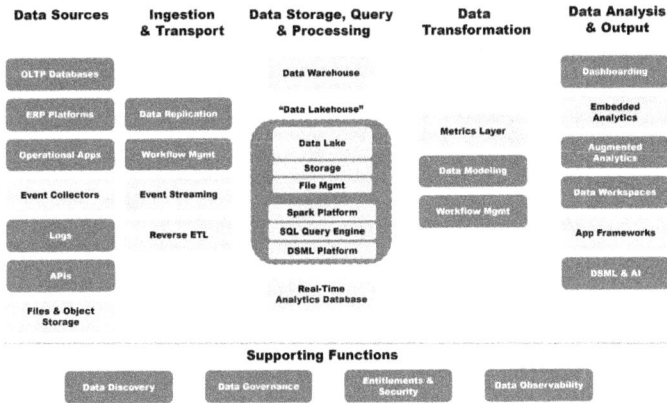

This book aims to help you understand these building blocks of data capability. This is so you get a handle on how the pieces fit together, which will help in deciding whether a one-size-fits-all approach from a cloud service provider might meet your needs versus the functionality/complexity tradeoff that comes from integrating multiple best-of-breed solutions.

Who Is This Book For?

This TinyTechGuide is for business, data, and technology leaders who understand the importance and potential value of data, analytics, and AI but don't quite see how it all fits together in the bigger picture.

The book is also for enterprise architects and technology architects looking for a primer on the data analytics domain, including definitions of standard functional components and usage patterns.

I also want to appeal to individuals early in their data analytics careers who wish to have a practical (and relatively jargon-free!) understanding of how all the "nuts and bolts" behind the scenes in a Modern Data Stack come together to turn data into actual business value.

Why Write this Book?

Suppose you want to lead or participate in initiatives that drive strategic decision-making, product innovation, or operational efficiency. In that case, data is your fundamental asset. It is at the heart of these endeavors.

Recognizing this fact, however, doesn't make it easy to get started.

A whole industry of data-tool vendors (over 1,400 at last count) has evolved over the past two decades, each offering unique solutions that promise to unlock the true potential of data to meet business challenges.[3] However, the competing claims of vendors have created enormous confusion and ambiguity, particularly for business leaders who may not be data experts.

I wanted to write a book that cut through this hype, providing strong foundational descriptions of each part of the Modern Data Stack to help leaders understand the underlying functional commonalities between different tools, making it easier to compare them and make better-informed decisions.

Rather than simply riding the wave of vendor hype, I wanted to break down each function and describe how it works, why it's needed (or not—this should not be a box-ticking exercise or shopping list), what alternative approaches exist, and what needs to be considered to make it part of a broader data strategy.

I also wanted to write a guide that explores the complete end-to-end supply chain for data: from raw, unrefined sources at one end to enriched, mission-critical decision material at the other. Whether data is the new oil, the new water, or the new bacon, the Modern Data Stack can be an engine to ignite innovation and drive success![4,5,6]

Practical Advice and Next Steps

The Modern Data Stack covers a lot of functionality and draws in a wide range of roles and responsibilities, from business domain specialists to technology experts.

Achieving success requires the following:

- **Obsessive focus on delivering business value**: Teams that generate value through the stack do so by focusing on the specific needs of an organization and adjusting course as needed.
- **A strong understanding of what's currently in place**: A good starting point is assessing current data infrastructure and identifying areas where modern tools can improve.
- **A resistance to vendor hype by undertaking independent research**: The Modern Data Stack isn't a one-size-fits-all solution. It's a collection of technologies, methodologies, and strategies that can be mixed and matched to cater to unique requirements. Research the tools available for each layer of the data stack, including taking advantage of trials and demos to better understand how they could meet needs.
- **A future-state roadmap blueprint**: Begin with a well-communicated technology and functionality roadmap that places scalability and future growth at the center of any planning assumptions.
- **An incremental approach, above all else**: Avoid a "big bang" approach. Instead, phase implementation, validate at each step, and iterate often. Complement this approach with frameworks like the observe-orient-decide-act loop (OODA) to manage the feedback from implementation decisions and plan next actions.[7]
- **An investment in people**: The Modern Data Stack is only sustainable when a team is trained and ready to adapt new technologies and capabilities into "business as usual" processes. A data-driven culture demands continuous learning and upskilling to properly realize the benefits of analytics at scale.

By the end of the TinyTechGuide, the reader will:

- **Understand the Modern Data Stack**: Learn the key concepts and terminology associated with end-to-end modern data architecture, from data ingestion to storage, processing, transformation, and analysis, while also covering key aspects of governance and security.
- **Know when to deploy critical data management functionality**: Understand the purpose, challenges, and implications of each element within the stack, and be able to differentiate between popular tools and technologies in these areas.
- **Learn to overcome implementation challenges**: Identify and address common challenges encountered when implementing a Modern Data Stack, such as data quality, latency, scaling, integration from multiple sources, billing, and security risks.
- **Understand future trends and innovations in data management**: Gain insights into the future of the Modern Data Stack, including trends such as addressing data silos, increasing self-service capabilities, and the emergence of data mesh and data products.
- **Receive Practical Guidance for Getting Started**: Learn best practices for implementing and optimizing a Modern Data Stack to improve decision-making, increase efficiency, and scale data-driven operations.

Summary

This chapter covered:

- The Modern Data Stack is a battle-tested architectural framework that provides a foundation for digital transformation.
- By adopting and integrating this stack, data leaders can improve their organization's capacity for better decision-making, efficiency, and competitive advantage.

- With the Modern Data Stack, organizations can handle increasing data volumes, integrate disparate data sources, and govern data more effectively using a flexible range of compatible technologies, often hosted in the cloud.
- This book aims to simplify a complex landscape of hundreds (if not thousands) of technology vendors by exploring each core function within the Modern Data Stack and integrating this into a broader data strategy. The aim is to help leaders make informed decisions beyond vendor hype.

Chapter 1 References

[1] Laney, Douglas. 2021. "The 18 Generally Agreed-upon Information Principles." LinkedIn. September 9, 2021. https://www.linkedin.com/pulse/18-generally-agreed-upon-information-principles-douglas-laney/.

[2] "Data Stack." Modern Data Stack. Accessed August 12, 2023. https://www.moderndatastack.xyz/stacks.

[3] Turck, Matt. 2023. "The 2023 MAD (Machine Learning, Artificial Intelligence & Data) Landscape." Matt Turck. February 21, 2023. https://mattturck.com/mad2023/.

[4] "The World's Most Valuable Resource Is No Longer Oil, but Data." *The Economist*. May 6, 2017. https://www.economist.com/leaders/2017/05/06/the-worlds-most-valuable-resource-is-no-longer-oil-but-data.

[5] Digital Bulletin. "Data Is the New Water." Medium. July 27, 2020. https://medium.com/digital-bulletin/data-is-the-new-water-62ed9bb5158a.

[6] Seiner, Robert S. "Data Is the New Bacon." *The Data Administration Newsletter*. November 15, 2017. https://tdan.com/data-is-the-new-bacon/18796.

[7] Wikipedia. "OODA Loop." Last modified December 28, 2003. https://en.wikipedia.org/wiki/OODA_loop.

Chapter 2

What Is a Modern Data Stack?

Tracing the Origins of the Modern Data Stack

The roots of the Modern Data Stack can be traced back 50 years or more to the advent of relational databases and data processing technologies in the 1970s.[1] However, the concept of a "modern" stack architecture began to take shape with the arrival of so-called "Big Data" in the early 21st century.

Figure 2.1: A Simplified Timeline to the Modern Data Stack

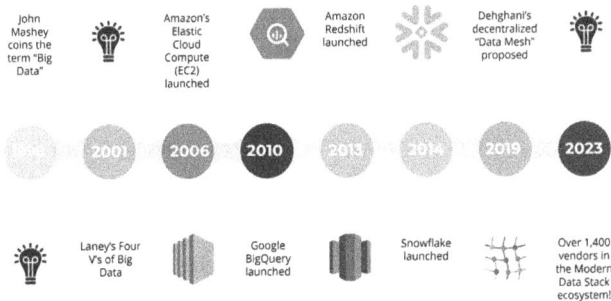

The term Big Data was first coined in the late 90s by American computer scientist John Mashey but was later popularized

by O'Reilly Media, an American publishing company.[2] The term came to represent the vast scale of data starting to be generated by businesses, electronic sensors, social media, and other sources. Traditional architectures like monolithic systems or earlier client-server models were insufficient to deal with this influx of new information.

The Four Vs

Analyst Doug Laney coined the Four Vs of Big Data—volume, velocity, variety, and veracity—in 2001.[3] This described the challenges associated with managing and analyzing large datasets and the concept has since become a vital and well-trodden way to characterize Big Data.

Table 2.1: The Four Vs

Concept	Why is it important?	How does the Modern Data Stack help?
Volume	The sheer mass of data generated and stored by organizations requires new storage, processing, and analysis approaches.	Provides robust, scalable, and flexible solutions for cloud-based data storage and distributed processing of large volumes of data.
Velocity	The pace at which data is generated and needs to be processed demands timely analysis for organizations to make informed decisions.	Stream processing and event-driven analytics solutions allow companies to analyze and act on data as it arrives for informed decision-making.
Variety	The different types and formats of data an organization might deal with—from structured relational databases to semi-structured emails and videos—require technologies to handle these other formats.	Data architectures can store raw data of any type, while modern approaches to processing allow this diverse data to be structured flexibly upon query, ensuring flexible analysis.

Veracity	The reliability or trustworthiness of data. Incoming sources might be incomplete or inconsistent and contain errors affecting the analytical results' accuracy. Data integrity through validation and cleansing is vital to maintaining high data integrity.	Integrated data quality and governance tools enable automated data cleansing, validation, and anomaly detection that help maintain data integrity, consistency, and confidence in our data through its journey.

Traditional data architectures began to struggle to deliver value when facing the challenges the Four Vs posed and this drove the new technologies and approaches that began to surface. Internet giants like Google and Yahoo drove this wave of innovation since they needed to store and analyze this emerging class of data while delivering global Internet search capability and digital ads to consumers.

The Arrival of Hadoop and NoSQL

A pivotal technology that emerged around this time was **Hadoop**, an open-source framework developed by a team led by Doug Cutting. This revolutionary technology allowed for distributed storage and processing of enormous datasets. Hadoop included two key components: the **Hadoop Distributed File System (HDFS)** for large-scale data storage and **MapReduce** for parallel data processing. Because of these innovations, Yahoo adopted Hadoop as the foundation of its search engine.

Outside of the dot-com giants, more traditional technology still held control. Since the 1970s, structured query language (SQL) has been the primary programming language for managing and manipulating relational database management systems (RDBMS) such as IBM's **DB2** or **Oracle**. SQL allows users to create, modify, and query databases using highly structured commands.

The early 2010s saw the rise of "not only SQL" (NoSQL) databases like **MongoDB**, **Cassandra**, and **Couchbase**. These addressed the perceived performance and scaling limitations with traditional relational databases in handling Big Data. NoSQL databases offered a more flexible, scalable solution for storing and querying *non-relational data*–that is, data not stored in traditional rows and columns within relational database tables.

An underlying flexible data-storage design sets NoSQL databases apart from their relational cousins. They could hold and process more diverse data types, which is especially useful for semi-structured data formats like JavaScript Object Notation (**JSON**) or eXtensible Markup Language (**XML**), where data structures could evolve or change significantly over time. NoSQL databases also prioritized query performance and low-latency data access, crucial for applications dealing with high data throughput or requiring real-time analytics.

NoSQL databases were designed with distributed computing in mind. They had built-in features like *replication*, which creates multiple copies of data for safety, and *sharding*, where data is distributed or split across multiple servers for efficient processing.

A distributed architecture improves overall system reliability and avoids a single point of failure within the system. These bottlenecks can cause the whole system to fail when a single element breaks down, making them highly undesirable for resilience and scaling.

Cloud Computing Meets Data Warehousing

Around the same time, the concept of cloud computing was gaining serious traction. The launch of **Amazon Elastic Compute Cloud (EC2)** in 2006 marked a significant milestone. EC2 provided scalable, on-demand virtual server instances to customers over the Internet and effectively launched the modern cloud computing era. Following Amazon's lead, other technology giants, notably Google and Microsoft, started offering their cloud computing services and platforms to businesses and individuals.

These developments set the stage for significant innovation in 2013 in the form of **Amazon Redshift**. This fully managed service, essentially an outsourced cloud-data warehousing solution, provides a way to analyze large volumes of data at a significantly lower cost than traditional on-site data warehousing platforms. With its worldwide scalability, high performance, and cost-effectiveness, Redshift quickly became a popular choice for data warehousing and analytics in the cloud.

While cloud-based data warehousing was gaining momentum, another significant development was taking place: the rise of **Apache Spark**. Originating as a research project at UC Berkeley's AMPLab, Spark offered improvements over Hadoop as a unified analytics engine for large-scale data processing and analytics. It was well-regarded for its speed and ease of use, shipping with built-in open-source libraries for *distributed machine learning* (training models using data across multiple computers) and *graph processing* (analyzing networks of data).

Thus, the mid-2010s marked the rise of modern data warehousing that is today the norm. Companies like **Snowflake** and Google (with its service **BigQuery**) joined Amazon Redshift in offering on-demand, scalable resources for data processing. Unlike traditional on-site data warehouses, where data storage and computing power were closely linked, these platforms separated both computing and storage. This separation allowed each to scale independently, offering a more flexible, cost-effective approach to data management and analysis.

Data Pipelines Feed the Cloud

As these data platforms became more established, a supporting ecosystem emerged that enabled data transport from external sources into the cloud for analysis. Data pipelines helped automate the process of data ingestion from transactional databases, business applications, and a wide variety of other sources. Vendors such as **Fivetran**, **Stitch,** and technologies like Apache **Airflow** (a project conceived initially at Airbnb) have become essential solutions for companies looking to extract and load data into these environments.

With large volumes of data arriving onto platforms, the concept of a "data lake" became a way to store and analyze data in its raw format without the expensive, time-consuming steps required to reshape and model the data into a more formalized data warehouse. Underlying formats such as **Amazon Simple Storage Service (S3)**, **Google Cloud Storage,** and **Azure Data Lake Storage** became common layers for receiving and storing ever-increasing volumes of raw data.

Over time, the data lake concept evolved, inheriting many traits of the traditional data warehouse, to become a "data lakehouse" that offers the best aspects of both data lakes and data warehouses: making it easy to ingest and store data from multiple formats—while also managing data structures—and enforcing data quality, security, privacy, and governance.

Visual and Collaborative Analytics Goes Mainstream

From the mid-2000s onwards, the business intelligence (BI) market was transformed. A new generation of tools prioritized interactive visual analytics over static, clunky operational reports, breathing fresh life into the industry. This new wave of software represented a significant shift, allowing data to be more easily understood and explored by a broader range of end users, thus enabling better decision-making.

Vendors such as **Tableau**, **Qlik**, and later, Microsoft's **Power BI** led this charge. Their distinction was to offer a new, user-friendly approach to data analytics known generally as "visual data exploration" with dynamic reporting and dashboarding that enabled users to combine data sources from on premises, the cloud, and hybrid data environments into a single view.

In parallel with these developments, browser-based notebooks like **Jupyter** became increasingly popular. Data scientists use these digital notebooks to write and run code, visualize results, and document processes.

Collaborative data science platforms, like **Databricks,** paved the way for more advanced analytics capabilities, exploratory analysis, machine learning (ML), and AI. Here, *exploratory analysis* refers to the initial process of analyzing data to find patterns or anomalies. At the same time, ML and AI involve training algorithms to learn from and make predictions or decisions based on data it has never encountered before.

Is Centralization the Answer? It Depends

As organizations' data needs grew more complex, the limitations of centralized data lakes and warehouses began to become apparent. While these systems have proven their value for storing and managing data, they often need help adapting to modern data usage's dynamic nature. In response, a new approach to data architecture was proposed: *the data mesh.*

Introduced in 2019 by Zhamak Dehghani (at the time, a principal consultant at **ThoughtWorks**), a data mesh shifts away from a "centralized" model (where all data is stored and managed in a single system) towards a "decentralized" one (where data management occurs across multiple systems).

A centralized data team is no longer solely responsible for delivering analytical data in a data mesh design. Instead, "domain teams"—groups with specific skills and expertise in certain areas of the data and its applications—take responsibility. Each team essentially becomes a "data product owner," a role that involves managing and refining their data, treating it as a valuable asset.

Other teams across the organization—and potentially even beyond the organization itself—consume this data, using it for their analyses and decisions. This approach empowers business and IT teams to work more effectively with the most relevant data while promoting more efficient use of resources across the organization by reducing bottlenecks in traditional data architectures.

Data mesh architecture is discussed further in Chapter 8.

Maturing Environments Lead to Maturing Practices

As the components of the Modern Data Stack ecosystem have developed, the focus has shifted towards enhancing the operational aspects of the end-to-end data lifecycle. This desire for improvement includes all stages, from data creation and collection, through processing and storage, to its ultimate analysis and use to drive business decision-making.

DataOps

DataOps has emerged as a practice emphasizing collaboration, automation, continuous integration, and deployment. The latter involves regularly merging code changes into a shared repository and automatically testing and deploying these changes, reducing the time it takes to improve and fix issues in the data process. By implementing DataOps practices, organizations can improve their data processes' efficiency and quality.

DataOps, while still in its infancy compared to the mature practice of DevOps, shares several tenets that can guide its development and ensure service and data availability, which leads to higher-quality project deliveries by delivering the following:[4]

- Focus on services rather than servers.
- Using infrastructure as code.
- Automating all processes.

Focusing on functional services, and not simply physical hardware, allows for various service-enhancing strategies like replication and failover, which can handle increased workloads and broad geographic distributions. Data should be viewed similarly, with a shift towards delivering data in multiple forms for various purposes. The range of analytics output will be covered in Chapter 6.

Implementing infrastructure-as-code (managing and provisioning computing resources through machine-readable definition files rather than physical hardware configurations) offers several advantages, such as quicker, error-free deployments and easy rollback of problematic updates. Infrastructure-as-code also applies to DataOps; all elements of data delivery must be captured in code to ensure predictable, reliable operations.

As will be discussed in Chapter 5, automation is key to maintaining service and data availability. Automated processes allow for smooth process management and timely responses to compliance violations, ensuring data freshness.

Just as a small DevOps team can manage large infrastructures with automation, a lean DataOps team can ensure data availability to dependent teams, applications, and services. These tenets underline the importance of an organized, automated approach to managing data in business, mirroring well-understood DevOps practices.

MLOps

At the same time, the continuous advancements in data science, machine learning, and artificial intelligence (DSML & AI) models have demanded the seamless integration of AI into operational processes. MLOps (also called ModelOps or even AIOps) has emerged to meet this need, ensuring these models operate smoothly and their scalability in a real-world setting.

This newer discipline tackles the challenges of managing ML models at scale, covering everything from model development (creating and training ML models) to deployment (implementing these models in a production environment) and ongoing updates and maintenance.

A Complex Modern Landscape

Today, the Modern Data Stack is a rich, complex tapestry of technologies and methodologies. It spans the entire data journey, from extraction-using tools like Stitch or Fivetran, through storage in data warehouses like Amazon Redshift or Google BigQuery, to transformation with tools such as **dbt**, and finally, analysis and consumption through business intelligence products like

Tableau, Qlik, or PowerBI and machine learning platforms like Databricks or **Dataiku**.

Despite its apparent complexity, it's the remarkable scalability, adaptability, and flexibility characterized in the stack that is described in this book. Its capability to handle various data types and a broad range of transactional and analytical use cases across industries sets it apart as an architecture that can help deliver significant value to the business through improved efficiency, innovative product development, and informed decision-making on large, diverse datasets.

Pay Attention to Functions, Not Vendors

So, for this TinyTechGuide, what's the best way to break down the Modern Data Stack into its underlying parts? If anything has been learned from the past two decades of data management technology, it's that change is inevitable. To paraphrase Ernest Hemingway, change in the data ecosystem happens two ways: gradually, then all at once.

To write a book on this subject, simply highlighting the current popular vendors won't serve the reader well over the long run. In 1958, the average tenure of a company on the S&P 500 was around 61 years. Recent analysis forecasts this to shrink to a span of just 15 to 20 years this decade, a trend that is likely to continue.[5] To describe the Modern Data Stack purely in terms of vendors would be pretty foolish, since many will fold, be acquired, or simply fade from view—while new entrants will capture market share and attention.

Instead, I'll take a *functional* perspective on the Modern Data Stack, highlighting the key capabilities that work together to deliver end-to-end business value. By breaking down a complex system into smaller, more understandable building blocks, it is possible to take a valuable, high-level tour of what data leaders need to know to implement a working, robust data analytics strategy that isn't driven first and foremost by vendor hype or product marketing.

What Is a Modern Data Stack?

Figure 2.2. **MAD Landscape in 2023**[7]

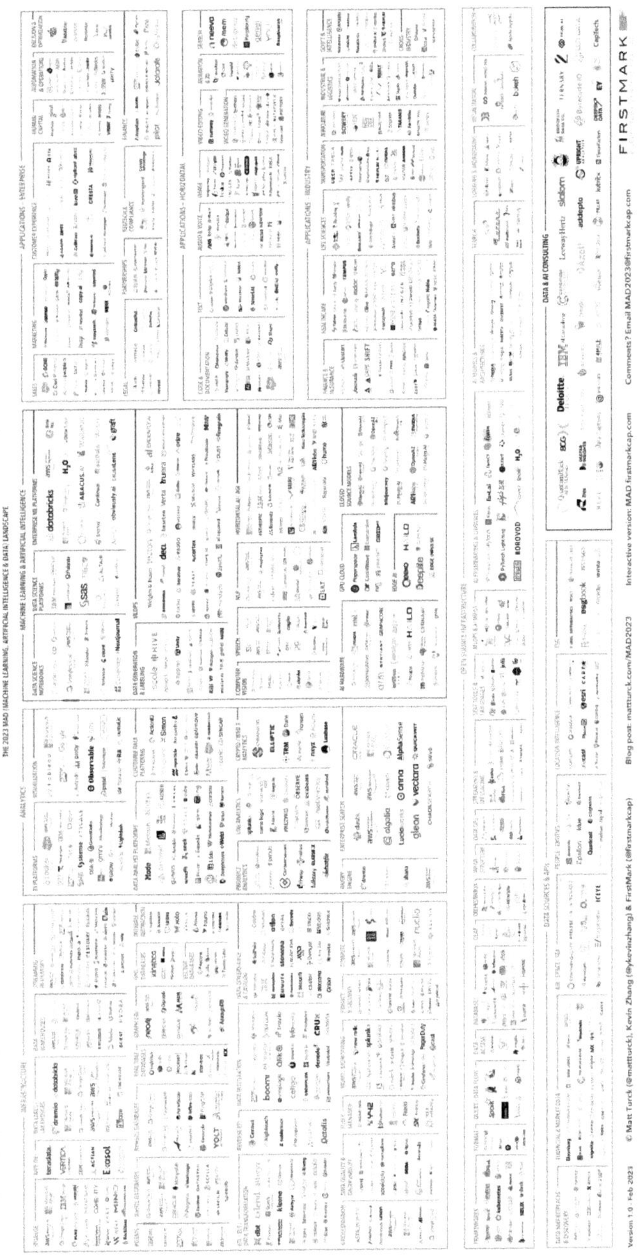

Of course, I'd be remiss if *representative* vendors in each function were not highlighted. But be warned, this list can't be exhaustive without becoming exhausting. When highlighting vendor maps like Matt Turck's machine learning, artificial intelligence and data (MAD) landscape, things can quickly get out of control.[6]

Instead, the functions considered in this book should have the benefit of a longer lifespan when it comes to building a resilient data analytics roadmap. Functional architecture is a blueprint for developing and implementing a Modern Data Stack strategy using one or more applications. Although individual vendors may come and go, our needs for data storage, transformation, and analysis will remain constant, at least at a high level.

Practical Advice and Next Steps

Getting started on the journey to a Modern Data Stack can seem overwhelming, given the sheer number of vendors competing for attention in this space. To start, consider the following steps:

- Talk to stakeholders to determine the most significant decision-making pain points and prioritize from there.
- Aim to build an incremental roadmap for functional capability—don't plan to boil the ocean with an overambitious plan that can't pivot or adapt to changing circumstances.
- Embrace the principle of "building for demise," where today's data architecture is simply tomorrow's legacy stack. Design and build using decoupled solutions that deliver capabilities that have clear functional boundaries and will be easier to maintain or replace in the future.
- Assess what kind of data an organization handles and the volumes or varieties associated with these sources.
- Understand an organization's appetite (or tolerance) for migrating data architecture to the cloud. Use this as a guide for considering cloud-service provider technologies or integrating several best-of-breed vendor solutions, considering factors such as scalability, cost, and a team's technical ability.

- Bake the idea of DataOps principles into designs early to improve collaboration and automation.
- Plan for continuous improvement. Keep up with evolving technologies and methodologies as the data landscape develops rapidly. Be ready to adapt a data strategy as needed.

Summary

In this chapter, the initial outlines of the Modern Data Stack were introduced, from its origins to what it looks like today. Although seemingly technically complex on the surface, the beauty of the stack lies in its adaptability and ability to grow with a business's needs.

There are many tech companies out there. Each shouts about their shiny new tool. It's easy to get dazzled and drawn into the hype. But here's a pro tip: don't just go by the brand name. Instead, get to know what these tools should be capable of—from pulling in data and storing it to reshaping it—and making sense of it all.

The tech world is constantly in flux. But there is one surety: we will continue to deal with ever-growing volumes and varieties of data. So, understanding these fundamental functions is a powerful advantage in building a future-proof data strategy. It's a roadmap to managing change and business expectations—no matter what comes next.

Chapter 2 References

[1] Kelly, Dan. "A Brief History of Databases." Cockroach Labs. February 24, 2022. https://www.cockroachlabs.com/blog/history-of-databases-distributed-sql/.

[2] Diebold, Francis X. "On the Origin(S) and Development of the Term 'Big Data.'" PIER Working Paper No. 12-037. https://doi.org/10.2139/ssrn.2152421.

[3] Patgiri, R., and A. Ahmed. "Big Data: The V's of the Game Changer Paradigm." IEEE Xplore. December 1, 2016. https://doi.org/10.1109/HPCC-SmartCity-DSS.2016.0014.

4 Palmer, Andy, Michael Stonebraker, Nik Bates-Haus, Liam Cleary, and Mark Marinelli. *Getting DataOps Right*. Sebastopol, CA: O'Reilly Media. https://www.oreilly.com/library/view/getting-dataops-right/9781492031765/.

5 Viguerie, S. Patrick, Ned Calder, and Brian Hindo. "2021 Corporate Longevity Forecast." Innosight. May 2021. https://www.innosight.com/insight/creative-destruction.

6 Turck, Matt, Kevin Zhang, and FirstMark. "The 2023 MAD (Machine Learning, Artificial Intelligence & Data) Landscape." Matt Turck. February, 2023. https://matturck.com/landscape/mad2023.pdf.

7 Turck, Zhang, and FirstMark. "The 2023 MAD."

Chapter 3

Data Begins Its Journey

Understanding Data Ingestion and Transportation

Our data architecture story starts with ingesting and moving data from various sources to the cloud, where it can be stored, processed, and used for analysis.

Effectively managing how data is gathered, transferred, and housed impacts everything from analytic reliability to systems performance to overall decision-making within an organization. In short, every application of analytics, data science, and so-called "systems of insight" lying downstream relies on this step for data delivery.

This process needs to be addressed in parts to break it down. First, the *data sources* will be discussed themselves to understand where the journey begins. Next, *data ingestion*, which is collecting and importing it into the central data stack, will be described. Finally, *data transport*—how to securely and efficiently move data from a source system to its target destination—will be explored.

Data Sources

Figure 3.1: Common Data Sources for Modern Data Architectures

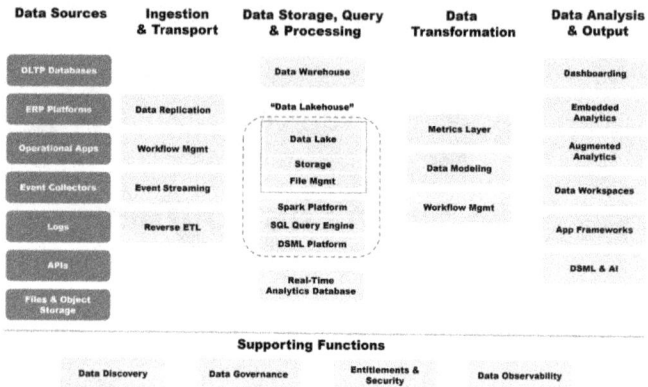

Data Sources	Ingestion & Transport	Data Storage, Query & Processing	Data Transformation	Data Analysis & Output
OLTP Databases		Data Warehouse		Dashboarding
ERP Platforms	Data Replication	"Data Lakehouse"		Embedded Analytics
Operational Apps	Workflow Mgmt	Data Lake	Metrics Layer	Augmented Analytics
Event Collectors	Event Streaming	Storage / File Mgmt	Data Modeling	Data Workspaces
Logs	Reverse ETL	Spark Platform / SQL Query Engine / DSML Platform	Workflow Mgmt	App Frameworks
APIs				DSML & AI
Files & Object Storage		Real-Time Analytics Database		

Supporting Functions

Data Discovery	Data Governance	Entitlements & Security	Data Observability

Online Transaction Processing (OLTP) Databases

Designed to handle real-time transactional workloads, OLTP databases capture, store, and retrieve data from typical day-to-day business operations data. Popular vendors for these technologies include Oracle, Microsoft (with their **SQL Server** platform), and the open-source **PostgreSQL**.

OLTP applications might consist of *e-commerce platforms* where customers place orders, resulting in database recording the transactions, updating inventory levels, and handling payment processing; *banking systems* that manage deposits, withdrawals, fund transfers, or account balance updates in real time; or *online reservation systems* used in the hospitality, travel, or transportation sectors that handle the real-time booking of flights, hotel rooms, or event tickets while ensuring data integrity, availability, and immediate confirmation of reservations.

ERP Platforms

These manage and integrate various business functions such as finance, human resources, inventory, supply chain, and more. These systems are usually large and complex, generating a wealth of operational data as businesses conduct day-to-day activities that follow different departmental processes. Sales orders, accounts payable/receivable, inventory movements, sub-ledgers, and customer-relationship management data are part of typical ERP platforms such as **Oracle ERP** or **SAP**.

Operational Applications

Applications such as **Salesforce** or **Hubspot** manage and track customer interactions, sales activities, marketing campaigns, and other operational processes. These applications generate vast amounts of data related to customer profiles, leads, opportunities, interactions, conversions, activities, and more.

Generally speaking, operational applications serve specific organizational functions, such as sales, marketing, customer service, project management, and e-commerce. Still, they can also offer specialized functionality in particular industries such as human resources (e.g., **Workday**), healthcare (e.g., **EPIC**), finance (e.g., **BlackLine**), or manufacturing (e.g. **Epicor**). They are often implemented as part of digital transformation programs to streamline manual operational processes, enhance customer engagement, or enable more efficient management of business activities.

Event Collectors

These capture and collect event-based data generated by systems, applications, or devices. An *event* can represent various activities, such as user interactions, system or application-level events, log entries, and Internet of Things (IoT) sensor data. These events are generated in real time when actions occur with associated systems or applications.

Event collectors play a significant role in *website analytics* (capturing page views, clicks, form submissions, or navigation patterns), *IoT data collection* (such as temperature readings, motion detection, energy consumption, or machine status), *application monitoring* (harvesting log files, error messages, or performance metrics), *cybersecurity* (examining network traffic, user authentication, or anomaly detection) and *social media monitoring* (processing events such as tweets, comments, shares, and likes).

Log Files

These may seem mundane as a data source for a cloud-based Modern Data Stack. Still, they serve a valuable purpose—capturing and storing a chronological record of important events, activities, and information related to systems, applications, servers, or individual devices.

Depending on the level of detail specified, log files may include error messages, user actions, system events, security alerts, or performance metrics. This information is generally stored for diagnostic analysis in the event of future issues. However, log files are often a valuable starting point for predictive analytics, such as anticipating a system failure.

Application Programming Interfaces (APIs)

APIs enable data access and integration between internal systems and external platforms or services. Through well-defined interfaces, APIs allow individuals or systems to interact and share data in a standardized and controlled manner.

For example, an organization may have an internal API that handles communication between its e-commerce platform and its inventory management system. The API can provide real-time updates on product availability, stock levels, or order information, allowing other systems to access and use this data in a well-understood way. External APIs work similarly but open up their functionality to a broader audience beyond an organization's boundaries, such as social media APIs, weather APIs, geolocation APIs, and many more.

Files

These represent the most common form of data storage in organizations. Information is arranged in hierarchical folders that mimic the physical binders and loose paper of decades ago.

Applications, systems, or processes commonly generate files, including spreadsheets, text documents, logs, images, videos, or sensor data. Typically, files store data in a format that is easily readable and understandable by humans and machines. However, sometimes files are stored in proprietary formats that are difficult to share.

Object Storage

In the context of the Modern Data Stack, object storage is a common data source that can manage massive amounts of data at scale and accommodate various types of data, especially semi-structured data source files. Cloud computing is used to deliver this scalability and flexibility.

Industries such as media and entertainment (for example, Netflix and Disney+) rely heavily on object storage to store and handle extensive volumes of multimedia content like video files, images, thumbnails, and metadata tied to their media assets. It is also an ideal choice for long-term data archiving and backup solutions because its scalability and durability make it suitable for retaining data over extended time periods while ensuring data integrity.

What Is Needed to Ingest and Transport Data?

Figure 3.2: Data Ingestion and Transport Functions

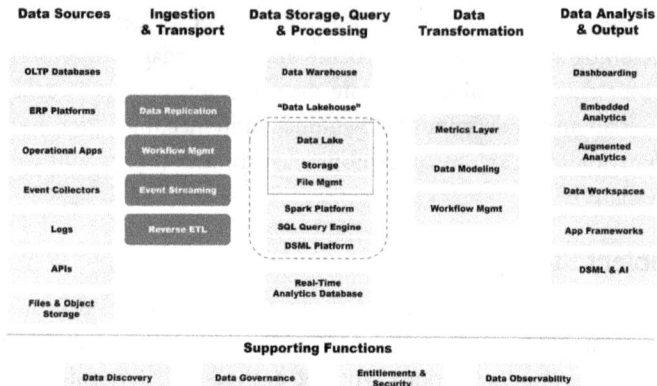

Data Sources	Ingestion & Transport	Data Storage, Query & Processing	Data Transformation	Data Analysis & Output
OLTP Databases		Data Warehouse		Dashboarding
ERP Platforms	Data Replication	"Data Lakehouse"		Embedded Analytics
Operational Apps	Workflow Mgmt	Data Lake	Metrics Layer	Augmented Analytics
Event Collectors	Event Streaming	Storage	Data Modeling	Data Workspaces
Logs		File Mgmt		
	Reverse ETL	Spark Platform	Workflow Mgmt	
APIs		SQL Query Engine		App Frameworks
		DSML Platform		DSML & AI
Files & Object Storage		Real-Time Analytics Database		

Supporting Functions

Data Discovery	Data Governance	Entitlements & Security	Data Observability

To transport data between source systems and intended destinations, data replication is required. This is essentially copying the original data in its original format to a logical depository known as a "staging area" for further processing, enrichment, and analysis. More about this will be discussed in later chapters.

Data replication doesn't occur in isolation. It's part of a larger ecosystem that requires a well-defined framework for workflow management that automates the data replication and movement steps, thereby reducing manual efforts and the potential for errors. Modern Data Stacks have workflow management capabilities capable for handling failures or exceptions, which ensures that disruptions to the data flow are managed effectively and quickly.

Incorporating performance metrics during these ingestion and transport steps is extremely important. It helps administrators understand how well the system's functions are performing and whether it's effectively handling the pressures of scale across large data pipelines. With effective workflow management, data leaders can proactively identify potential bottlenecks or issues before they escalate, enabling them to maintain the system's uptime, efficiency, and reliability.

Data ingestion and transport functions create a strong foundation for any Modern Data Stack. They ensure that data is collected efficiently and consistently, forming the basis for an organization's insights, analyses, and strategic decisions.

However, several situations can disrupt these processes or cause them not to work as expected. Let's break these down.

Disruptions in Data Pipelines

Before diving into the various data pipeline capabilities, let's examine some factors that can (and often do) cause them to break down. It's important to be aware of these issues so that planning scenarios and remediation mechanisms to detect and minimize disruption can be created.

- **Inconsistent or Unreliable Data Sources**: Tools and technologies for data ingestion and transport rely heavily on the reliability and consistency of the source data. When these fail, it can result in missing or inaccurate data, which affects data replication and transport processes to subsequent processes in the stack.
- **Changing Source Data Formats**: Synchronization between ingestion and transport tools and the formats and layout of source data systems is critical. Any misalignment between the source and target can cause disruptions or inaccuracies in the data movement process and other downstream issues.
- **Connectivity Issues**: Any disruptions or instabilities in the connections between technology solutions and data sources can interrupt data processing. This definition includes Internet outages and bandwidth limitations that slow down data transfer speeds, which will lead to potential data pipeline bottlenecks. As will be discussed shortly, handling the restart of a data pipeline following a disruption requires almost as much consideration as "business as usual."

These potential issues underscore the importance of implementing adequate data ingestion and transport processes and continually monitoring and optimizing them to ensure their reliability and efficiency.

> **Fast-Track Integration: A Peer-to-Peer Lending Firm's Rapid Journey to Optimized Data Migration**[1]
>
> A financial services firm specializing in peer-to-peer lending used these capabilities as a vital tool for syncing their data from various third-party sources (including Salesforce, HubSpot, **Intercom**, and **Google AdWords**) into their Redshift data warehouse.
>
> The choice of data ingestion and transport tooling was driven by the need for high compatibility with their data sources and cost-effectiveness for data migration. They could set up and configure these components within a few days, using dbt for their production models—saving the company significant time and costs compared to in-house development.
>
> They also found value in "webhook" functionality (allowing lightweight, event-driven integration and transport between two systems via an API) and are planning to push data to Amazon S3 with increased usage of **Redshift Spectrum**.

Data Replication

Data replication ensures that businesses have the most up-to-date information available for analysis and decision-making. Indeed, most Modern Data Stacks rely heavily on efficient data replication.

Our key challenges in data replication typically fall into four main categories:

1. Dealing with different data formats.
2. Ensuring data consistency.
3. Managing data replication in increasingly small-time windows.
4. Handling large volumes of data.

A successful data-replication strategy must address these challenges by providing comprehensive data transformation capabilities, consistency checks, and handling the volume and velocity of incoming data sources.

Change Data Capture: Tracking Updates in Data Sources

Change data capture (CDC) is the primary data architecture pattern for replicating data into the Modern Data Stack. It's a routine that efficiently identifies and captures changes in data so that replication can efficiently process data that has changed, delivering the results to other components in the stack.

Traditionally, data was transferred in bulk from databases to data warehouses using *batch schedules* on a monthly or weekly basis. However, with businesses' growing demand for data analytics, these batches are now usually processed nightly or within shorter windows. These *batch windows* became a significant source of tension for data teams since increasingly large volumes of data from various systems must be transferred within an ever-shrinking timeframe.

If batches failed to be completed within their allotted time, the process would cause significant delays in data availability for downstream analytics and reports. Worse yet, a batch failure would present data leaders with difficult decisions. Should they attempt to rerun a batch job during traditional working hours—potentially straining the performance of live business applications—or should they let the business operate without the updated data and "fly blind" until the next day's batch run?

CDC allows data teams to make data-replication processes more efficient, selectively ingesting and transporting only those records that have changed since the last batch-processing run. For example, in a hypothetical database of 1 million records, perhaps only 5 percent would have been updated since the previous batch window.

The computation effort required for the data replication of 50,000 records is significantly less than what's needed for the entire 1 million record dataset. In this way, CDC enables near real-time replication by dealing with only a relatively small proportion of the data.

However, CDC is not a one-size-fits-all solution. For large, static datasets that require full reprocessing, CDC may not be the most efficient method. Also, implementing CDC requires great care to prevent data loss, duplication, or out-of-order processing—especially in distributed environments.

Let's explore the high-level steps of CDC in leading software technologies such as Fivetran or **Matillion**.

Figure 3.3: Example of a CDC Process

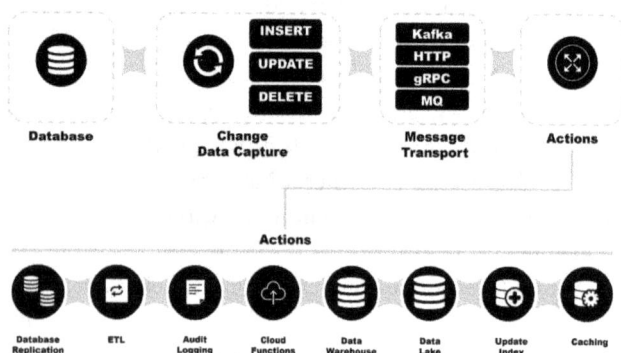

First, a data source is needed, usually a relational database like PostgreSQL, **MySQL,** or any other platform that can store data and register transactional changes in the data.

CDC implements a process for change detection, monitoring the data source for alterations. A change could be an event like a database trigger firing due to a data element being created, updated, or deleted.

Changes are commonly detected by querying tables for records that were last updated during a specific time range; for instance, all sales records that were updated in the previous twenty-four hours. Another method is to ingest and analyze transaction log files for a more "forensic" examination of changes, such as in the case of debugging a faulty data pipeline or auditing a potential data breach. The techniques used will depend on what the data source supports and the capabilities of the CDC tools.

Once changes are detected, they must be recorded. This process often involves staging the changes in an intermediate area in the data architecture or writing them into a job queue for processing.

Metadata, such as the timestamp of the change, the type of change recorded (e.g., inserting, updating, or deleting a record), and the state of the data before and after the change itself are added during the recording process.

Recorded changes typically include metadata such as the time of change detection, the type of change (e.g., record insertion, update, or deletion), and the state of the data before and after the change.

Captured changes are delivered to the target system, usually located elsewhere within the stack. These changes are generally directly applied by the CDC software, but can also be formatted to allow the target environment to apply them instead.

CDC demands robust error handling and recovery mechanisms to ensure no data is lost. For instance, if a change fails to apply in the downstream target environment, the CDC system might retry the operation, send an alert, or log the error for later analysis.

This strategy has several advantages over the traditional batch-processing approach to data replication. CDC allows data updates in near real time and reduces source systems' computational load and network bandwidth usage.

Near real-time updates mean intraday data replication during business hours is feasible without significantly impacting overall system performance. Also, it enables a history of data changes to be maintained, which is crucial for auditing and robust data governance.

Seamless Data Replication for a Leading Sales Engagement Platform[2]

When a leading sales engagement platform faced challenges around how to merge distributed tables in Amazon Redshift for in-depth analytics, they turned to change-data replication to centralize their data and build out stronger customer usage insights.

Their CDC strategy involved creating separate database areas for each distributed source, and then merging them into a single unified view within their cloud data warehouse. This method bypassed the complexities of more traditional ETL pipelines and ensured that any new or altered data was automatically updated and available in a central location for analytics.

As will be covered later in this chapter, CDC is an important enabler for event-driven data architectures designed to respond quickly to business events and real-time analytics.

Developing a Data-Replication Strategy

This involves balancing the costs and benefits of various factors.

Begin by defining the primary business objectives for data replication. While this may seem rudimentary, it's an important step. Is replication required for disaster recovery, data accessibility, or to enhance data analytics within the Modern Data Stack? A data-replication strategy that aligns closely with stakeholder objectives and requirements will be more effective.

Remember, not all data requires replication. Identifying which does and how to transport it to the target destination is crucial. Implement a data classification policy that prioritizes high-value data, which enables smarter, cost-efficient decisions that will minimize the data stack's operational budget.

Pro Tip:

Determining Which Data Requires Replication and Transport

- **Talk to Stakeholders**: What looks like a pure technology problem is often a "people" problem. Different stakeholders will have different views on which data is essential. These views must inform and shape the replication strategy.
- **Identify and Understand the Business Processes behind the Data**: A holistic view of where data comes from requires an understanding of the processes that caused its creation or movement. Data associated with critical processes will likely be the highest priority for replication.
- **Make a Risk Assessment**: What's the potential impact on a business if data is lost or unavailable at key moments? For example, suppose it's the month's end and the chief financial officer (CFO) needs to close the books within three working days. In that case, there's both an operational impact (e.g., disrupted business processes) and a strategic impact (e.g., regulatory, compliance, or loss of commercial advantage). Prioritize data ingestion and transportation accordingly to address these risks.
- **Consider the Data Lifecycle**: Some data has extreme short-term value, but this may decrease over time. Prioritize rapid delivery of this data over other performance parameters to maximize benefits. Also, consider using a tiered storage strategy in overall data architecture, where replicated data is readily available for a certain period before being moved to more cost-effective, slower-access storage. Cloud service providers offer a wide range of data options that need to be considered "hot," "cool," "cold," or "glacial" at different times in the lifecycle.

There's a wide range of options for implementing data replication, from snapshots and transaction replication to merge replication. Sophisticated CDC data ingestion may be unnecessary for smaller data volumes. On the other hand, a simple batch process might not suffice for a nightly load pipeline that runs to millions of data rows. Tailor a strategy to specific needs, and remember that one size does not fit all.

A forward-thinking data-replication strategy will account for the potential data source and volume growth. The system's design must scale with increasing data and changing business needs.

Regular monitoring, auditing, and testing of the data-replication process is vital for promptly identifying and correcting issues. Consider various scenarios in which a replication process could fail at different points in the pipeline. Understand the risks and the necessary mitigation and recovery steps for each potential failure.

Data security and governance are paramount. Replication tools may gain privileged access to sensitive data and create additional copies. It's crucial to ensure that data-replication software adheres to all necessary regulations and security policies at every step of the data ingestion and transport process.

Workflow Management

Once key data-replication processes are in place, an effective workflow management strategy for ingestion and transport is essential. Handling data pipelines is a continuous task, not a one-time event. Therefore, automating and managing these pipelines, ensuring data integrity, and making workflows scalable, reliable, and efficient should be considered when planning successful data architectures.

Much like a symphony, data workflows must be well-orchestrated to function smoothly. Each step in the workflow can be represented as a node in a process flow diagram, also known as a directed acyclic graph (DAG). This visualization allows us to see the dependencies between tasks and ensure data is processed in the correct order.

Figure 3.4: Example of a Directed-Acyclic Graph (DAG) for a Managed Data Processing Flow

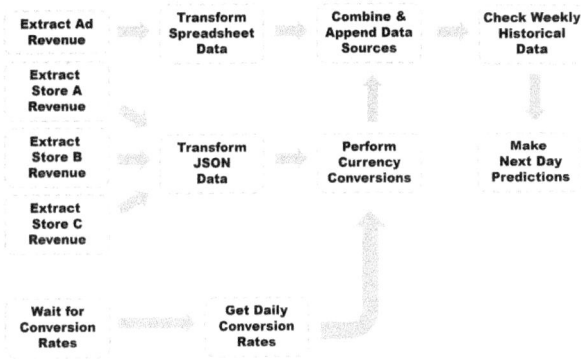

The first step in creating a workflow management strategy involves understanding the source data, its formats, and update frequency. This understanding allows the design of efficient workflows tailored to the data.

Data validation tasks are crucial to ensure the quality of the ingested and transported data, including its accuracy, completeness, consistency, and validity. These checks provide reliable data for downstream processing.

An effective workflow strategy should include mechanisms to detect and respond to failures and errors. An operational runbook (a step-by-step guide for the tasks required to perform and maintain operational activities) might involve automatically rerunning the process if specific errors are encountered or sending alerts for manual intervention. Proactive monitoring is vital for timely issue detection and resolution. As workflow management matures, alternate processing paths for specific failure conditions can be included, allowing for more sophisticated error handling.

Workflow management also requires continuous improvement. Regularly reviewing workflow performance to identify bottlenecks or inefficiencies, and encouraging a culture of issue detection and resolution, can keep workflows optimized as data and demand scales.

How to Manage Data Moving in Real Time

Unlike traditional batch processing—which typically involves scheduled transfers of data—event streaming captures, analyzes, and responds to data immediately. It is beneficial for managing fast-moving events such as user interactions on websites or applications, sensor readings, and financial transactions.

Event streaming unlocks the value of fast-paced data, providing real-time insights and allowing immediate action—this ability to react in real time offers a significant competitive advantage for businesses.

However, developing an event streaming strategy requires careful planning. The complexity of event-based data capture can lead to higher costs than batch data movement. Additionally, it may require specialized data architectures—like microservices (independent components of an application) or message queues that handle communication between different services—to deliver a scalable solution.

Several technologies are available for event streaming, each with strengths and weaknesses. **Apache Kafka** has gained popularity within the open-source community due to its high data throughput, which means it can process many real-time events, and also its fault tolerance capabilities. However, commercial platforms may provide performance and support benefits over open-source solutions.

Revving Up Data: How a German Automaker Streamlined Real-Time Information[3]

A major German car manufacturer needed to make real-time data, generated by its production facilities and sales network, available to anyone across the global business. They initially turned to open-source Apache Kafka but found it operationally challenging to meet service levels.

To address this, the manufacturer worked with **Confluent** to deliver a data streaming platform that would accelerate the internal use of Kafka and support continuous innovation and new use cases by offering easy access to data as real-time streams.

This resulted in access to real-time data, a reliable, zero-downtime data streaming platform, and full integration with existing SAP solutions, industrial IoT protocols like **OPC UA**, and enterprise-wide cloud applications and services.

If an organization is a heavy user of a specific cloud service provider, it's likely they offer an event-streaming component. For instance, **Amazon Web Services (AWS)** provides **Amazon Kinesis**, and Azure offers **Event Hubs**. Other providers have unique advantages, such as tiered storage or more robust data management through message queues.

When collecting and processing data events, maintaining data consistency is crucial to ensure all subsequent parts of the data stack can read the flowing data.

To facilitate this, define a data serialization format like JSON, XML, or Avro. These formats help systems parse, interpret, and exchange information more easily. Also, a schema registry is used to help manage and validate schemas for data quality (consistency) and data governance (validation and compliance). The schema can also track changes to the data over time, particularly as data structures evolve to include new attributes or relationships.

Given the rapid nature of event streaming, any issues can quickly impact the entire system. Therefore, designing a reliable, fault-tolerant architecture incorporating design patterns like replication, failover, or recovery strategies is critical. Tracking the health and performance of the event streaming platform is equally essential. Use monitoring tools to track metrics, log data, and trace system processes to detect real-time issues.

Event streaming is a technically complex discipline. The consumers of streaming data will likely be software developers and analytics engineers rather than business users directly. Aim to make it as easy as possible for these technical users to work with event streaming via good documentation, friendly APIs, and developer tooling to access the latest streamed data.

Building Resilience: A Global Advisory's Leap to High-Availability[4]

A global investment advisory company partnered with AWS to construct a multi-region data infrastructure solution for their Enterprise Advice service. This solution was needed to ensure high data availability and minimal replication lag for seamless failovers in case of primary region service failure.

The setup relied heavily on Amazon Kinesis to capture and stream large quantities of data from multiple sources in real time. The solution also used **AWS Lambda** to replicate data from the Kinesis data streams in the primary region to a secondary one, ensuring the system's resilience and efficiency.

Amazon DynamoDB global tables were used for replication checkpoints to prevent data duplication and facilitate data streaming resumption from the last checkpoint. Vanguard used an additional tool, **Qlik Replicate**, for their CDC processing, which was deployed on Amazon EC2.

The solution could automatically switch from the primary to the secondary region when encountering service issues, minimizing data loss and maintaining data ingestion capabilities. This robust architecture aided the company by enhancing the resilience of its workloads and meeting its high-availability goals.

Reverse ETL

Reverse ETL, an emerging component in the Modern Data Stack, addresses a growing need for operational systems to directly access enriched analytical data from the data warehouse, data lake, or data lakehouse.

This approach involves taking output data from these storage layers; enriching, blending, or standardizing it; and *pushing it back* into operational systems like CRM, marketing, content management, or sales platforms. This data augmentation step can improve decision-making, automate business processes, and increase efficiency.

Designing a reverse ETL strategy begins with identifying a clear business case. Answer questions like:

- "Which operational systems require access to enriched analytics?"
- "How often should this data be updated?"
- "How will this enrichment add value to operations?"

Answering these questions might involve improving data quality in CRM systems, identifying high-value segments for marketing automation, or personalizing user experiences.

Data pushed back into operational systems must be carefully mapped and transformed to align with the system's data schema. Implementing data validation checks is also crucial, as is choosing a platform capable of managing various data delivery scenarios, such as updating existing records or creating new ones.

Reverse ETL can be complex due to the intricacy of operational system databases. Therefore, collaboration between data teams and functional teams is critical. Errors in the reverse ETL process should be effectively handled by being identified and isolated for future attempts.

One must also consider the implications of reverse ETL for change management. Changes in the data stack or the receiving source systems can affect reverse ETL workflows, making it crucial to have a robust change-management plan. Further, consider how reverse ETL could impact data governance, and ensure that all data flowing back into operational systems complies with relevant policies and regulations.

Practical Advice and Next Steps

- **The Importance of Up-Front Planning**: Remember, the foundations of the entire data stack depend heavily on the performance, efficiency, and reliability of the data ingestion and transport strategy. Choosing the right tools, setting up appropriate processes, and continuously monitoring data pipelines for potential issues should be at the forefront of planning.

- **The Diverse Nature of Data Sources**: Be prepared to handle different types of data, from structured transactional data to unstructured log files and event data. A flexible and adaptable data ingestion and transport strategy is critical here. Each data source may require unique handling, extraction, transformation, and loading processes.
- **Clear Processes for When Things Go Wrong**: Make sure to include error handling, recovery, and reprocessing in the case of disruptions. Once in place, continuously monitor the performance and health of data pipelines. Watch for potential issues such as slow processing, failed jobs, or data quality issues.
- **Sharpen the Saw**: Use monitoring insights to continuously optimize data ingestion and transport processes. Look for bottlenecks, inefficiencies, or points of failure and work to mitigate these issues.

Remember, with the Modern Data Stack, the data journey is as important as the destination. Early in the process, proper data handling will set the stage for a successful data journey.

Summary

It's crucial to remember that the functions of data ingestion and transport form a cornerstone in the building and maintenance of a modern data architecture.

With data replication, workflow management, and event streaming, each aspect is critical in helping organizations acquire and manage data for later processing and analysis. Developing a strategy is vital for handling large data volumes within tight, high-pressure time windows. It's essential to understand the complexities and nuances of approaches, which depend on business objectives, the situational nature of the data, and a forward-thinking approach that prepares for the expanding scale and evolving requirements of business stakeholders.

Remember the importance of error handling and recovery mechanisms in these processes. Ensuring data security and maintaining strict governance over data is paramount when dealing with ingestion and transport.

Progressing into subsequent chapters, the architectural components of the Modern Data Stack that heavily rely on the principles discussed in this chapter—including efficient and scalable data storage, processing, and analytics—will be explored.

Chapter 3 References

[1] "Growth Street Saves Time and Money Replicating Data to Redshift." Stitch: A Talend Product. Accessed August 12, 2023. https://www.stitchdata.com/customers/growth-street-saves-time-money-replicating-data-to-redshift/.

[2] Enriquez, Elvia Loya. "Replicating Sharded Databases: A Case Study of SalesLoft, Citus Data and Fivetran." Fivetran. Accessed August 12, 2023. https://www.fivetran.com/case-studies/replicating-sharded-databases-a-case-study-of-salesloft-citus-data-and-fivetran.

[3] "Revving up IoT Use Cases with Real-Time Hybrid Cloud Data Architecture." Confluent. Accessed August 12, 2023. https://assets.confluent.io/m/5d747e088352cf08/original/20220825-CS-BMW.pdf.

[4] Boppanna, Raghu, Parameswaran V. Vaidyanathan, Mithil Prasad, and Richa Kaul. "How Vanguard Made Their Technology Platform Resilient and Efficient by Building Cross-Region Replication for Amazon Kinesis Data Streams." AWS. February 23, 2023. https://aws.amazon.com/blogs/big-data/how-vanguard-made-their-technology-platform-resilient-and-efficient-by-building-cross-region-replication-for-amazon-kinesis-data-streams/.

Chapter 4

How to Store, Query, and Process Data at Scale

The heart of the Modern Data Stack lies in its ability to store, query, and process data for analysis in a central, scalable location.

As was covered in Chapter 3, organizations collect vast and varied information from multiple sources, such as transactional databases, logs, sensors, and social media, each with different formats and schemas. However, the real challenge lies in not only collecting this data but storing it in ways that are readily accessible and usable across the entire organization to enhance decision-making, accelerate processing, and reduce costs.

The Modern Data Stack addresses this challenge by offering a centralized storage system capable of handling large volumes of data, streamlining management, and facilitating data mining for insights. Analysts can answer intricate business questions by enabling complex queries over large datasets. At the same time, data teams carry out heavy data processing tasks to transform, aggregate, and reshape data for a myriad of business outcomes.

In this chapter, the significant components in this part of the stack will be unpacked. The evolution of the traditional data warehouse (which offers structured storage for processed data as it moves from on premises to the cloud) and the rise of the data lake (for raw data storage and analysis and its recent metamorphosis into the data lakehouse, which merges features of both predecessors) will be explored.

The concept of real-time data—a crucial aspect in today's business environment that enables instant decision-making, real-time analytics, and improved customer experiences—will be revisited. How storage, querying, and processing are handled differently for this high-value, high-velocity data category will be explored.

Figure 4.1: Typical Functional Components for Data Storage, Query, and Processing

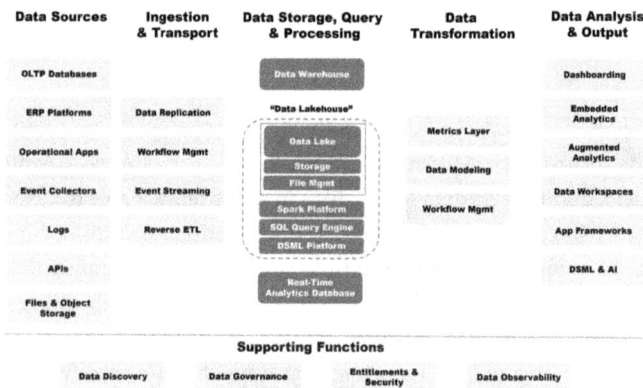

Data Sources	Ingestion & Transport	Data Storage, Query & Processing	Data Transformation	Data Analysis & Output
OLTP Databases		Data Warehouse		Dashboarding
ERP Platforms	Data Replication	"Data Lakehouse"		Embedded Analytics
Operational Apps	Workflow Mgmt	Data Lake	Metrics Layer	Augmented Analytics
Event Collectors	Event Streaming	Storage	Data Modeling	Data Workspaces
Logs	Reverse ETL	File Mgmt		
		Spark Platform	Workflow Mgmt	App Frameworks
APIs		SQL Query Engine		DSML & AI
		DSML Platform		
Files & Object Storage		Real-Time Analytics Database		

Supporting Functions

Data Discovery	Data Governance	Entitlements & Security	Data Observability

Data Warehousing: The Early History

Let's take a little stroll through recent data management history to understand how the current landscape took shape.

Data warehousing is a concept that has been around for several decades. The term was initially coined by Bill Inmon in the 1970s and has been defined as a "subject-oriented, integrated, time-variant and nonvolatile collection of data" supporting decision-making processes.[1]

In the early days, the primary purpose of the data warehouse was to centralize data from multiple sources—transforming it into a framework suitable for reporting and analysis. Because of the longer-term nature of the data collected, companies used data warehouses to analyze historical context, trends, or patterns for crucial business processes.

Early implementations were typically hosted on premises, i.e., installed and run on computer servers in an organization's managed data centers. With storage and computing power at a premium, these solutions were often expensive and complex, requiring significant investments in hardware, software, time, and technical expertise.

As the concept of business intelligence gained traction in the mid-to-late 1990s, data warehousing had a resurgence after Ralph Kimball proposed a new approach to implementation known as "dimensional modeling."[2]

With this approach, data warehouses deconstruct into smaller "data marts" that each focus on one specific business process and create integrations through shared, conformed business definitions ("dimensions") that were heavily reused between data marts. This led to consistent reporting and analysis.

Approaches to modeling data in a stack will be covered more extensively in Chapter 5.

From On-Premises Storage to the Cloud

With the rise and rapid growth of the Internet and e-commerce, traditional on-premises data warehouses struggled to handle the explosion of data resulting from online transactions and the arrival of widespread "Big Data," as discussed in Chapter 2. This led to the emergence of cloud-based data warehouses, which were flexible, scalable, and often more cost-effective than their on-premises predecessors because they didn't require businesses to maintain their own hardware.

Leading from the Cloud

At the time of this writing, leading cloud data warehouses include:

- **Google BigQuery**: Launched in 2010, it provides a fully managed, serverless data warehouse with a flexible, pay-as-you-go model.
- **Amazon Redshift**: Launched in 2012, offers a data warehouse service that integrates with existing business intelligence tools. Known for petabyte-scale implementations that are backed by Amazon's cloud storage capacity and high-speed analysis of large datasets.
- **Snowflake**: Generally available in 2015, offers a unique architecture that separates storage from computing resources and has focused heavily on building a strong partner-led data ecosystem.

Planning a Modern Data Warehousing Strategy

The design of an optimal cloud-based data warehouse strategy must consider the changing landscape of data analysis and management, from the Modern Data Stack components described in this book to planning for future disruptive innovations.

These days, it's rare to start a data warehousing project without a legacy data architecture as the foundation. A clear understanding of business needs is vital to guide the rest of the strategy. Will a cloud-based data warehouse be responsible for migrating data from older systems? Will those systems be demised (switched off) due to this strategy to save the organization money?

Despite having a reputation for being globally available, some important geographical considerations are needed when planning for a cloud-based data warehouse. Choosing a cloud region that is geographically closer to users or applications will minimize network latency and enhance the overall performance or responsiveness of the warehouse. Not all cloud services and features are available in every region, so ensure that specific services (for example, managed data warehouses or analytics tools) are compatible with the regions being considered. Likewise, ensure that privacy obligations and regulations for each potential region are also understood, as these can differ widely worldwide.

Cloud service providers may have varying pricing models based on the region chosen, and it's important to realize that transferring data between regions can incur additional, unexpected costs. It's critical to assess these costs as part of a longer-term budget forecast.

Distributing data across multiple regions can provide redundancy in disaster recovery. If one region experiences an outage or some disruption, failover to another region to ensure uninterrupted access to data is possible.

Game Changer: Transforming Fan Data Management in US Sports[3]

A major US sports league needed a more efficient method for managing a large volume of fan data generated by digital and in-stadium transactions. This was essential for product feature development, personalized content creation, and connecting fans with the sport.

The customer managed over 350 legacy data pipelines from third-party and internal sources to a central enterprise data warehouse. This system was plagued by inefficiencies and operational challenges.

After an evaluation process, the league migrated to Google Cloud's BigQuery. Tasks included data replication, ETL conversion, report conversion, end-user training, and security configuration. The project was completed in seven months.

The migration brought several benefits, including cost savings with BigQuery's on-demand pricing model, improved query performance, and better integration with other functional components within this architecture.

Post-implementation, the customer managed and analyzed large volumes of fan data more efficiently, reduced operational overhead, and improved performance as processing moved closer to real time. These improvements are now powering personalization features and insights for better fan experiences.

The Impact of Data Gravity and Governance

Data warehouses are a tremendous source of "data gravity" where, as data accumulates and grows in volume, it becomes increasingly difficult and costly to move to different locations or cloud providers.

Since a data warehouse often forms a core component within a Modern Data Stack, the destination that drives business value—usually analytics, data science, and AI—must always be kept in mind, as covered in Chapter 6.

Data Gravity: A Force to Be Reckoned With

This is almost a natural law in a data ecosystem: just as larger objects exert more gravitational pull in the physical world, the greater the volume of data in a warehouse, the more applications, services, and analytics it attracts.

As data accumulates, it often becomes tightly coupled with specific cloud services and infrastructure. There is a resulting loss of project agility to adopt new technologies and cloud providers and scale infrastructure as needed.

Data gravity can also increase vendor lock-in risks, making migrating from one provider to another challenging. The cost and complexity of moving large volumes of data, re-architecting applications, and retraining staff can make switching vendors financially and operationally prohibitive. Unfortunately, this can lead to a dependency on a single provider and the risk of "price gouging" in future contract years.

Is there a roadmap for analytical maturity due to data processing on this new centralized data store? What current and future analytics are needed from this data warehouse? To maximize the return on investment for stakeholders, consider everything from legacy report migration, self-service query, and analysis to more advanced analytics and AI strategies.

As the data volumes and varieties grow, it becomes more important to have a robust data governance plan in place (covered in Chapter 7). Data governance puts controls in place to unlock how data is published and made "findable" within an organization, control who has access to what data, how to determine the correct use of data, and how to ensure its quality.

To mitigate the risks associated with data gravity and vendor lock-in, consider implementing data management practices that promote data portability, such as containerization (covered in Chapter 8), open standards, and cloud-agnostic architectures to minimize future lock-in as warehousing scales.

Remember, the goal of a modern data warehouse strategy should be to effectively turn data into insights, enabling data-driven decision-making that drives a business forward. To determine whether a data warehouse strategy is effective, track a range of key performance indicators (KPIs) related to data quality, query performance, user adoption, and data integration efficiency to assess strategy effectiveness:

Table 4.1: Key Performance Indicators for Measuring Data Warehouse Effectiveness

KPI Category	Indicator	Purpose
Data Quality	Data Accuracy	Compare back to trusted golden sources or conduct periodic audits.
	Data Completeness	Tracks the percentage of complete data records, ensuring that essential fields are populated.
	Data Consistency	Ensure conformity of data arriving from different sources.
Query Performance	Query Response Times	Measure the average query response against periodic benchmarks.
	Query Execution Plans	Track the query execution logic to ensure sufficient resources or optimization.
	Query Complexity	Track the average number of joins, subqueries, or aggregations to identify future performance bottlenecks.

User Adoption	User Engagement	Measure the frequency and duration of user interactions with the warehouse, including daily/monthly active users.
	User Feedback	Collect feedback through surveys or interviews to assess user satisfaction.
	User Self Service	Track the percentage of users who use self-service capabilities to analyze their data without direct IT/technology intervention or support.
Data Integration Efficiency	Integration Time	Measure the time to integrate new data sources into the data warehouse.
	Integration Success Rate	Track reliability and effectiveness of data integration workflows.
	Integration Cost	Evaluate the cost associated with data integration, including any ETL processes

The Emergence of the Data Lake

Traditional data warehouses were primarily designed for well-understood, relational data that fit into predefined data structures. However, in recent decades, the explosive growth in semi-structured data (which only loosely includes a predefined form, such as social media data, sensor data, log files, documents, etc.) led to the emergence of a new class of data architecture for storage, query, and processing: the data lake.

Think of a data lake as an expansive attic or basement in a home. Just as one might store all kinds of items in the attic—boxes of old clothes, furniture, books, childhood mementos, and much more—a data lake is where businesses can store all their raw data, irrespective of the source or format.

Just as stored items may be organized or chaotic, with clear labels or none, information in a data lake can range from highly structured to completely unstructured. And much like someone might one day sift through stored items, discovering long-forgotten treasures or essential documents, businesses can dive into their data lake to unearth insights and value whenever necessary.

But remember, if not correctly managed or cataloged, finding what is needed in a cluttered attic—or a poorly organized data lake—can be daunting.

Data warehouses typically follow a *top-down approach* where data is pre-modeled and collected for specific use cases. This design approach can lead to performance and agility bottlenecks when data arrives in more varied forms, as this work needs to be done up front before any analysis can be started.

On the other hand, data lakes offer a *bottom-up approach*, storing vast amounts of raw data in various formats without needing pre-modeling or transformation. When a data team wants to explore or experiment with data in this format, the data is reshaped or remodeled—but only at this point—allowing for more agile analytics that directly answer pressing business questions.

Unlike traditional databases or data warehouses, a data lake does not need to understand what data it receives before storing it. This means virtually any type and amount of data can be poured into the lake in real time and processed later as needs dictate.

To describe the components of a data lake, let's talk about the specifics of data storage and data processing at scale.

How Is Data Lake Storage Organized?

Scalable storage solutions such as a Hadoop Distributed File System (HDFS) are typically the basis for most data lakes. Data is organized in hierarchical folders, similar to Windows Explorer or Mac's Finder.

Object storage has recently gained popularity due to its ability to handle vast amounts of unstructured data in a flat structure, facilitating search and scalability. Prominent examples of object storage include Amazon S3, Google Cloud Storage, and Azure Blob Storage.

Figure 4.2: Data Lake Formats, Storage, and Management Architecture

Data Lake Formats	Data Lake Storage	Data Lake Management
Delta	CSV	AWS S3
Iceberg	Avro	GCS
Hudi	Parquet	ABS
		HDFS

The Types of Data Stored in a Data Lake

By design, data lakes can accommodate virtually any type of file, spanning text files (ranging from simple CSV formats to more complex XML or JSON structures), log files, images, videos, binary files (files containing binary data), and even data exported from databases in diverse formats.

These different formats organize and compress data for storage in the data lake. Each approach has unique strengths and weaknesses, making them more or less suitable for various workloads.

CSV Files

These files are straightforward and well-understood—you've probably used one recently. Each line in a CSV file represents a record, with each field in the record separated by a comma or another textual delimiter. While CSV files don't have built-in mechanisms to define the type and structure of data or compress data (meaning that files can become extremely large for more extensive datasets), they're an excellent choice for simple, human-readable formats, especially if storage space isn't a significant concern.

Avro Files

Avro is an open-source file format that stores data in a row-based format like CSV. It offers the advantage of embedding a structural definition of the data within the file, making Avro a good fit for data that may evolve, such as when new fields are added to the data due to application enhancements. Avro supports compression through various technologies ("codecs"), each offering different efficiency and performance trade-offs.

Parquet Files

A popular open-source file format, Parquet organizes data by column rather than row. This makes Parquet particularly efficient for analytical querying, where typically interest is in only a subset of the columns, making it a common choice for analytics storage in the Modern Data Stack. Parquet has broad support and strong integration across popular data processing frameworks, including open-source Apache technologies such as Spark, **Hive**, **Impala,** and **Arrow,** as well as commercial offerings from **Dremio**, **Starburst**, and **Incorta**.

Parquet supports schema evolution and compression similarly to Avro. Still, it differentiates by offering "predicate pushdown," which is a way to quickly retrieve the needed data in a query and improve performance by skipping over irrelevant data storage.

Processing in the Data Lake

By offering scalable storage of raw, unprocessed data in diverse types and formats, data lakes differentiate from legacy data warehouse architectures. Moreover, they enable the processing of this data using various technological frameworks capable of distributing their workload across large networks of economical, commodity machines.

This contrasts with traditional data warehouses that often require expensive and proprietary storage and processing hardware, making data lakes a compelling proposition for analyzing large data volumes.

MapReduce

One of the earliest processing frameworks for data lakes was MapReduce, first introduced by Google and later popularized by Apache Hadoop. It is a batch-oriented model designed to process large datasets by dividing tasks into two principal phases: the "Map" phase and the "Reduce" phase.

- In the "Map" phase, data is parsed and transformed in parallel across multiple nodes in the data lake, creating an intermediate dataset. This dataset is then sorted (or shuffled) across the nodes, preparing it for the final analysis stage.
- The "Reduce" phase involves executing analytical functions such as summarizing, aggregating, filtering, or joining these sorted intermediate datasets. The results are then consolidated and written to an output file or another data storage system, which is the outcome of the MapReduce job.

MapReduce was praised for its fault tolerance and scalability, which enabled it to manage massive datasets. However, in today's data landscape, it's primarily considered a historical footnote. Faster, more straightforward frameworks—like Apache Spark—have superseded MapReduce, offering more efficient processing for a broader range of workloads, especially for iterative or interactive data tasks.

Spark

Seeing the limitations of MapReduce in terms of speed, ease of use, and flexibility, researchers sought to develop a more capable platform. In 2009, the University of California (UC) Berkeley's AMPLab began developing what would later become Spark.

Spark's core features an in-memory computing engine for high-performance distributed data processing. Spark introduced the concept of Resilient Distributed Datasets (RDDs), an immutable and fault-tolerant data structure.

Being *immutable* means that once an RDD is created, its content cannot be changed. This property allows for greater consistency, optimization, and parallel processing during data processing tasks.

Fault tolerance in Spark pertains to its ability to recover data during a processing failure. Spark can rebuild any lost RDD partitions by re-executing the transformations on the available data, with immutability simplifying fault recovery by eliminating the need to track changes.

Spark was swiftly open sourced, catalyzing its widespread adoption through community contributions. Its versatility, speed, and suitability for various data processing workloads garnered significant industry attention. Soon, Spark became a top-level Apache Software Foundation project, a testament to its maturity and credibility.

Over time, Spark has matured into a swift, general-purpose cluster-computing system. It provides high-level APIs in popular languages like Java, Scala, Python, and R. It supports a rich set of high-level, more accessible tools such as **SparkSQL** and **DataFrame API** for structured data processing, **MLLib** for ML, **GraphX** for graph processing, and **Structured Streaming** for real-time data processing.

In today's data landscape, Spark is not just a replacement for MapReduce. It has become a robust, comprehensive ecosystem supporting processing, analytics, and ML tasks. Its extensive capabilities and flexibility make it a popular choice in distributed computing.

Major Spark Platforms

While it's entirely possible to set up and configure an open-source Spark platform without licensing costs, many organizations prefer to use a managed Spark platform provided by a vendor. These platforms simplify setup, scaling, operating, and supporting a production-ready Spark framework.

Below is a brief comparison of some of the leading Spark platforms currently on the market.

- **Databricks**: Established by the original creators of Apache Spark, Databricks provides the Unified Analytics Platform (UDAP) as a cloud service. UDAP offers a collaborative workspace designed for data engineers and data scientists.

Databricks has pioneered the "data lakehouse" concept, combining traditional data warehousing and data lakes. Databricks is an excellent choice if directly seeking cutting-edge, unified analytics solutions from a development team that includes Spark's creators.

- **Amazon Elastic MapReduce (EMR)**: As a part of Amazon Web Services (AWS), Amazon EMR provides a fully managed environment for running Spark on AWS-hosted cloud infrastructure. It integrates seamlessly with other AWS services, such as S3 storage and various AWS data stores. If already an AWS user or looking for a platform that offers tight integration with other AWS services, Amazon EMR could be a solid choice.

- **Azure Synapse Analytics**: This platform provides dedicated Apache Spark compute capabilities via "pools," which are provisioned on demand, allowing Spark workloads to run within the Synapse Analytics environment. As with other platforms, Azure Synapse Analytics integrates closely with data lake storage, enabling Spark jobs to access large volumes of data in a single environment. If heavily invested in the Microsoft ecosystem, this platform can offer tight integration with an existing infrastructure.

Where's My Spark for Snowflake?

While Spark currently doesn't run directly on Snowflake, there are alternatives available.

Snowpark (we'll leave it to the reader to decide if this is an anagram of "Spark now" or not) allows analytics engineers and developers to write code in their preferred language (Scala, Java, or Python) and execute it directly within Snowflake. It aims to provide a familiar DataFrame API for data transformation and manipulation, similar to the developer experience with Apache Spark.

How Spark Gets Implemented

Implementing a Spark-based data processing strategy involves a strategic approach and careful consideration of various factors. Here are some essential steps to follow:

- **Integration with Existing Components**: Spark strategies are not developed in isolation. Consideration of how it fits into an existing data stack is crucial. If previously invested in cloud services like AWS, Azure, or Google, then choose Spark platforms that integrate with these services to optimize resources.
- **Align Business Requirements with Spark Capabilities**: Leverage Spark's various components for different needs. Use SparkSQL for structured data processing, Structured Streaming for real-time event processing, and MLLib or GraphX for ML and graph processing tasks. Ensure choices align with business and data processing requirements.
- **Ensure Data Security and Compliance**: With large data volumes and complex workloads, planning for data security and compliance early in the project lifecycle is crucial. Implement security measures such as data encryption, user authentication, and access controls. Remember, enterprise-grade security features provided by platforms like Databricks, Amazon EMR, or Azure Synapse Analytics can be invaluable for data protection—whether at rest or in motion.

When Data Lakes Fail: Data Swamps

The fundamental aim of a data lake is to store raw data, but maintaining organization is essential to prevent it from becoming a "data swamp."

A data swamp is an unmanageable, disorganized data lake that is difficult to navigate or use effectively—essentially a failure of the data lake strategy.

Outlined below are several issues that can contribute to the spread of a data swamp.

- **Poor Data Governance**: The absence of well-defined data quality standards and robust data stewardship can lead to a cluttered data lake filled with inconsistent, low-quality, or irrelevant data. The inability to locate and trust the data reduces confidence in the data lake.
- **Data Inconsistency and Silos**: Poor data quality is often a result of insufficient data cleansing or validation during data ingestion or transportation to the data lake. Varying data formats, missing values, or conflicting data attributes only add to the chaos. This issue compounds when different teams ingest and store data independently without proper coordination or adherence to data integration practices, leading to data silos.
- **Lack of User Adoption**: A data swamp can also represent a "people problem." Analysts may need more skills or knowledge, with adequate training and support, to use the data lake effectively. Failure on these fronts results in underutilization and a pileup of unexplored data.

Although real-life examples of data swamps are scarce (perhaps due to companies' hesitancy to share their data management failures?), it's important to remember that a data swamp's formation is often noticed only when it's too late. Hence, a continuous improvement program is necessary to prevent a data lake from degrading.

Organizations should establish robust data governance practices, enforce metadata management, ensure data cleansing, and uphold data integration processes to avert the risk of a data swamp. It's equally crucial to invest in user training and promote data literacy. These proactive approaches will help unlock a data lake's full potential and prevent it from becoming a data swamp.

When Data Lakes and Warehouses Converge

The decision to use either a data lake or a data warehouse can hinge on several factors. Each has its own advantages and trade-offs. Decision-making should be driven by the need to align with an organization's specific needs.

Data lakes are known for their cost-effectiveness and can store a wide variety of data without pre-processing or structuring. Their scalability is another advantage, allowing for adding new sources and types of data, thereby keeping pace with the dynamic data landscape.

On the other hand, data warehouses provide superior performance for querying and analysis due to their preprocessed and structured data. This makes warehouse architectures ideal for applications requiring near real-time performance, such as business intelligence or analytics. Data warehouses are often more secure, designed to store sensitive data explicitly, and meet compliance requirements for specific applications.

However, these strengths and weaknesses are not set in stone. An organization's particular needs and strategy should be the guiding factor rather than strict allegiance to one dogmatic approach.

This has led to the emergence of the "data lakehouse" architecture. This concept merges the advantages of data lakes and data warehouses, aiming to provide a unified, scalable solution for data storage, querying, and processing. The data lakehouse represents an evolution in data management strategies, symbolizing the convergence of these two traditionally separate approaches.

The Data Lakehouse

Lakehouse architecture represents a pivotal innovation in data management. It combines a data lake's storage scalability and data diversity with a data warehouse's transactional consistency, performance, and user-friendly features.

Let's dive into its essential components:

- **Unified Storage**: As its foundation, a lakehouse adopts the data lake's scalable and cost-effective storage system, which is often based on object storage. This unified storage allows a lakehouse to ingest and store a broad spectrum of data types for subsequent querying and processing, ranging from raw, structured, semi-structured, and unstructured data.

- **Schema Enforcement**: In a critical distinction from traditional data lakes, a lakehouse implements a data structure during data querying, not necessarily during ingestion. This hybrid approach allows data ingestion without an enforced structure. Still, it ensures that when queries execute, they operate on a well-defined schema, providing high-performance analysis without sacrificing the flexibility of data ingestion.
- **Transactional Capabilities**: In a significant departure from established data lake architecture, a lakehouse introduces transactional capabilities to data management—enabling atomicity, consistency, isolation, and durability (ACID; see box below) properties for data modifications.

ACID Transactions: Explained

ACID is a cornerstone in data management, ensuring data reliability and integrity, an acronym for:

Atomicity: Guarantees a transaction is treated as a single, undividable operation. All changes made by a transaction are committed together or not at all. This ensures consistent data states, even amid failures or interruptions.

Consistency: Enforces that a transaction will bring the database from one consistent state to another. This means it must meet a set of predefined rules or constraints. Any changes must be rolled back to maintain data integrity if a transaction breaches any constraints.

Isolation: Ensures concurrent transactions don't interfere with each other. Each one operates as if in isolation, even when numerous transactions run simultaneously. This prevents data inconsistencies from concurrent access, ensuring consistent and predictable transaction execution.

Durability: Promises that, once a transaction is committed, its changes are permanently captured in persistent storage, such as a disk or solid-state drive, to withstand subsequent system failures.

Introducing ACID transactions into a Modern Data Stack isn't without trade-offs. There's a performance cost due to locking, isolation, and commit protocols. Early data lake architectures focused on high throughput and parallel processing, which may be impacted by enforcing ACID transactions.

However, enabling ACID transactions in the data lakehouse architecture is a significant leap towards achieving a balanced blend of data warehouse performance and data lake flexibility.

- **Compute Layer**: Responsible for processing and analyzing data in the lakehouse. It enables users to execute SQL queries, conduct analytics, and develop ML models directly on raw data. Schema enforcement capabilities govern all these operations. Apache Spark is often the go-to framework in this layer, but there are alternatives, such as **Trino** and **Presto** (explored later in this chapter).
- **Metadata Management**: Can encompass various types of information about the data—including its structure, quality, and lineage—which provides information on its source and post-processing destination, among other details. The lakehouse architecture emphasizes strong metadata management to track and organize data across the platform. Treating metadata as a first-class citizen in a lakehouse means prioritizing it and using it as a pillar for data discovery, governance, and trust. In this context, a "first-class citizen" refers to an entity that supports all the operations generally available to other entities, including being passed as an argument, returned from a function, and assigned to a variable. By applying this to metadata, its importance and usability within the lakehouse structure is emphasized.

Data Reshaped: A Financial Giant's Leap to Lakehouse for Rapid Insights[4]

A large European financial services company sought to transition from a legacy data warehouse system to a modern, data-driven model to better leverage their large-scale data for strategic decision-making and operations. To achieve this, they established a cloud-based, domain-driven lakehouse and a data mesh approach, allowing for more efficient and collaborative data workflow among their team of over 500 data professionals.

Their use of the Databricks Lakehouse Platform enabled them to operationalize and democratize data across their organization, providing simplified access to various data sources and manageable infrastructure at scale.

By incorporating Delta Lake, they created fast and reliable data pipelines, crucial for their analytics and data science teams. The company's data analysts performed analytics on the lakehouse using PowerBI, while data science teams could quickly deploy models into production using MIflow.

The transition to Databricks resulted in multiple operational improvements, such as faster response to customer preferences, enhanced fraud detection using ML, and improved business operations through more efficient customer support. The bank has delivered dozens of use cases at ten times the speed of its previous infrastructure, with plans for further significant growth.

How a Data Lakehouse Handles Transactional Work

In recent years, several critical open-source technologies have offered ACID transactions, scalable metadata handling, and unified batch and stream processing on top of traditional data lake storage.

An overview of these technologies includes:

- **Delta Lake**: An open-source storage layer developed by Databricks. Built atop Apache Spark and Parquet, it's fully compatible with Spark for querying and processing data.

- **Delta Sharing**: A secure data-sharing protocol, also designed by Databricks. This standard allows for the secure, governed, real-time sharing of large datasets across organizations—independent of the computing platforms used. While it works well with Delta Lake, it is considered platform-agnostic.
- **Apache Iceberg**: Iceberg is another open-source table format for high-volume, slow-moving tabular data, designed to enhance the decoupled storage-and-compute model of a data lake. Like Delta Lake, it provides ACID transactions and scalable metadata handling. Furthermore, Iceberg isn't tied to any particular compute engine, allowing a variety of engines (Dremio, Spark, Trino, and others—even Snowflake) to read Iceberg tables simultaneously.
- **Apache Hudi**: The acronym for Hadoop Upserts Deletes and Incrementals, Hudi hints at its capabilities. Initially implemented by Uber to manage large-scale data needs, it introduces stream-like capabilities to batch-like datasets.

These technologies aim to augment data lakes with additional features that form the core of modern data lakehouse architectures. Features such as *transactional consistency*, *schema evolution*, *upserts* (a term for updating or inserting new or changed data), and *time-travel querying* (which allows data analysis when it was stored at specific past points) are notable among these.

The choice of integrating these capabilities into a lakehouse strategy will depend on specific needs and the ecosystem in use. For instance, a significant prior investment in Apache Spark might naturally lead to the selection of Delta Lake due to its deep integration with this technology stack. **Apache Iceberg** is a good fit for more computing-agnostic architectures, while **Apache Hudi** is an excellent choice for record-level inserts, updates, and delete operations.

Querying the Lakehouse: SQL Engines

Opening the lakehouse to query and analysis is the start of the journey to unlocking the full potential of the data inside the platform. Historically, relational databases and data warehouses used SQL as a readable and intuitive language to query, analyze, and explore connected datasets. This trend continues in the Modern Data Stack.

By seamlessly integrating SQL engines with the lakehouse, companies can harness the capabilities of these engines to query and analyze vast amounts of data in a transactional and versioned environment without requiring significant upskilling of their data analyst teams, since they will likely have familiarity with SQL.

From the earliest data lake implementations, SQL allowed a more comprehensive range of users to access and explore their data without resorting to code-heavy Java- or Scala-based engineering scripts.

Apache Hive, developed by Facebook engineers in 2008 and later open-sourced to the Apache Software Foundation, was a data warehousing infrastructure based on the Hadoop platform. It introduced a query language, **HiveQL**, that converts SQL-like queries into MapReduce jobs for large-scale data processing. As a result, Hive allowed SQL-savvy users to interact with Hadoop more easily.

In 2012, Cloudera introduced Impala, an open-source, massively parallel processing (MPP) SQL query engine for Hadoop. Impala aimed to provide real-time, interactive SQL queries directly on Hadoop data, eliminating the need for more time-consuming MapReduce jobs and improving query performance using in-memory processing and columnar storage.

Also in 2012, Facebook developed and released Presto as an open-source distributed SQL query engine for high-performance and interactive analytics across multiple data sources, including Hadoop, Apache Cassandra, and more. Presto gained popularity for its ability to handle large-scale data processing with low latency.

In 2013, Incorta released the Direct Data Mapping technology, enabling analysts to directly query and analyze raw, unprocessed data from complex business applications without transformation or traditional data processing.

A Direct Data Mapping engine preprocesses this raw data to determine all potential query paths through the data's original structure. This allows Incorta to execute queries directly on raw data without transforming or aggregating it. For data sources that include ERP applications (where the underlying database may include thousands of individual, relational tables), this can be a significant query accelerator versus the traditional extract, load, and transformation processes currently in common use.

In 2019, the Presto project underwent a significant transformation and rebranding, with a group of engineers from the Presto community forking the project and creating an independent open-source project named Trino. Starburst, founded in 2017, focused on further developing and commercializing this technology to provide additional features, enhancements, and enterprise-grade support for Trino deployments.

Dremio, launched in 2017, has been key in advancing the Apache Arrow project—an in-memory data format designed for quick and efficient data interchange across different systems. In 2019, Dremio made its platform open-source, encouraging community contributions and enhancements to the data processing engine.

In 2021, Databricks introduced **Photon**, a new vectorized query engine crafted to boost the performance of Spark SQL and DataFrame API queries. The term "vectorized" refers to a type of query execution that processes multiple rows of data simultaneously, leading to significant improvements in the performance of large queries. Photon's additional ability to cache frequently accessed data further enhances performance.

Various query engines now process data in lakehouse architectures. These engines have taken traditional SQL—the common language of data analysts—as their starting point, offering evolutionary improvements over time.

However, there is no universal choice for an SQL query engine within a data lakehouse. Evaluating multiple engines is crucial to consider their performance and compatibility with a data stack architecture. As technology evolves and needs change, be open to reassessing choices and switching to a superior option if available.

Data Science and Machine Learning in a Lakehouse

The final cornerstone in lakehouse architecture is the ability to power data science, ML, and AI workloads.

Data science, an interdisciplinary domain, employs scientific methodologies, processes, and algorithms to glean insights from structured and unstructured data. As strictly a branch of data science, ML harnesses statistical techniques to enable machines to enhance their performance on specified tasks over time.

AI embodies a machine's capability to undertake learning and decision functions typically associated with human cognition. These capabilities are honed and validated through data science and ML.

For a more in-depth exploration of this subject, consider *Artificial Intelligence: An Executive Guide to Make AI Work for Your Business* (part of the TinyTechGuide series).

DSML & AI capabilities are supported directly in the query and processing layer of the Modern Data Stack, i.e., the core functionality described in this chapter. These are distinguished from end-user tools that generally use *refined* data—produced after multiple sources have been transformed and curated—which are integral to delivering DSML & AI capabilities. This functionality will be covered in more detail in Chapter 6.

Python Frameworks

DSML & AI platforms usually incorporate popular open-source libraries and frameworks to enhance flexibility and power. For many organizations, Python is the preferred programming language for these capabilities.

Python's versatility as a general-purpose language is undeniable. It's equally effective for development, scripting, automation, and more, making it an adaptable tool for diverse sets of tasks. With clear and intuitive syntax that is user-friendly, it enables data scientists and engineers to swiftly write robust code for intricate systems.

Most crucially, Python boasts a rich ecosystem of libraries and frameworks for data analysis, visualization, ML, and beyond. Its widespread use in academia implies that new algorithms often become accessible with Python interfaces before this occurs in other languages, offering business teams an early entry point to groundbreaking research.

Deep Learning Frameworks

The origins of artificial neural networks can be traced back to the 1950s and 60s. Due to constraints in computational power and data availability, progress largely stagnated until the 1980s and 90s, when significant strides were made in learning algorithms and neural network architectures.

The term "deep learning" was first introduced to the ML community by Rina Dechter in 1986 and subsequently to artificial neural networks by Igor Aizenberg and colleagues in 2000.[5,6] The field experienced a pivotal moment in the mid-2000s when large-scale, end-to-end models became viable due to advancements in hardware (such as GPUs), increased data availability, and the advent of effective neural network training techniques.

Since then, deep learning has delivered state-of-the-art results in various domains, including image recognition, speech recognition, natural language processing (NLP), and many more.[7] The emergence of powerful deep learning frameworks in recent years has significantly contributed to these accomplishments by making complex models more accessible to build, train, and deploy.

Generative AI

The origins of generative AI (genAI) can be traced back to the initial stages of AI research, where simple generative models were employed for basic tasks like generating random numbers. However, the introduction of the Generative Adversarial Network (GAN) by Ian Goodfellow and colleagues in 2014 propelled the field forward.[8]

GANs position two neural networks against one another–a *generator* that fabricates new data instances and a *discriminator* that attempts to discern whether these instances are authentic or fabricated.

As a result of numerous evolutionary iterations, the generator progressively enhances its ability to create new data that can deceive the discriminator. The end product is data so convincingly accurate that it could easily fool a human observer into believing another human crafted it.

In recent years, transformer models like GPT have demonstrated impressive capabilities in developing human-like text. Introduced in the paper "Attention is All You Need" in 2017, transformer models produce sequence-to-sequence tasks such as machine translation, text generation, and named entity recognition.[9] By encoding each word in the context of all other terms in a sentence, they effectively handle long-range relationships in the text.

Although generative models are a relatively new addition to AI, they have already found many applications. From creating art and music to generating realistic human faces to aiding drug discovery—the growth and development of this field have been significantly driven by powerful and user-friendly frameworks like **ChatGPT**, **DALL-E,** and **Midjourney**.

Incorporating DSML and AI Processing into a Modern Data Stack

The choice of data science and ML components largely depends on the specific problems that need to be solved. Various platforms are tailored to address different issues. For example, PyTorch and Tensorflow are typically used for deep learning tasks such as image or speech recognition. In contrast, Dask and Ray are better suited to scale Python code across a machine cluster.

While some platforms have steeper learning curves than others, it's vital to choose frameworks that not only possess the necessary DSML capabilities but also prioritize user-friendliness and code readability. It's also beneficial to look for platforms backed by a substantial community, as this can make finding support and troubleshooting resources easier.

While exploring model building, validation, and deployment in depth in Chapter 6, remember that data science, machine learning, and artificial intelligence are still rapidly evolving fields. Teams should commit to ongoing education and prepare to re-evaluate platform choices as the landscape progresses regularly.

Real-Time Analytics Databases

In most architectures, data is traditionally gathered over a specific time frame before being processed and analyzed in batches. As discussed earlier, there's a growing need for businesses to have immediate access to the most current data. This trend leads to a significant reduction in the time window for processing these batches.

To cater to this need within the Modern Data Stack, real-time analytics databases can process and analyze data as soon as it enters the stack, which offers immediate insights.

Such components support near-instant data querying and analytics, thereby enabling businesses to respond to changes and make decisions based on the most current data. This real-time capability is crucial for use cases such as fraud detection, event monitoring, and delivering instant customer recommendations.

There are four main ways to compare the capabilities of a real-time database against their more traditional variants:

Table 4.2: Capabilities of Real-Time Databases vs. Traditional Databases

Criteria	Real-Time Database	Traditional Database
Data Freshness	Provides immediate insights from data as it gets ingested.	Operates on batch schedules. Data is not usually available immediately.
Data Latency	Very low (typically, milliseconds).	Variable, but usually hourly or nightly as part of a batch window.
Complexity	Requires more complex data architecture and management to handle streaming data and deliver insights.	Generally, more straightforward and well-known data architecture.
Costs	Expensive due to streaming infrastructure and instant querying.	Usually cheaper and commoditized.

Real-Time Data Architectures

The demand for real-time data access and processing has grown substantially in recent years, making selecting an appropriate database architecture crucial. Several key architectural components must be considered when designing a database for real-time access.

These include adopting data streaming or event-driven architectures, in-memory storage for faster data access, effective indexing to enable quick data retrieval, strategic data partitioning and sharding, and columnar storage for efficient data management.

We'll briefly explore these components to understand their roles in shaping an efficient real-time database:

- **Data Streaming/Event-Driven Architectures**: As covered in Chapter 3, these databases ingest data using stream processing frameworks such as Apache Kafka or Amazon Kinesis rather than awaiting data delivery in batches. An event-driven architecture allows these systems to respond to incoming data through events or messages from source systems. When evaluating options, consider their ability to handle late-arriving data and manage structured, semi-structured, and time-series data. This latter aspect is particularly vital in use cases within the financial services sector.

- **In-Memory Storage**: To provide immediate access, real-time databases store data in memory (RAM) instead of disk storage. Memory access is significantly faster and offers ultra-low latency for read/write operations.
- **Indexing**: Indexes are data structures that enable the database to swiftly locate required data without scanning each record. Like data, real-time databases also hold indexes in memory, resulting in rapid queries and data lookups. Modern databases support various indexing mechanisms—including bitmap, inverted, and star-tree indexes—to optimize query patterns.
- **Partitioning and Sharding**: Distributing data across numerous nodes, or shards, allows a database to reduce the data amount a query needs to search. Additionally, it spreads out (parallelizes) the query's execution across multiple similar nodes, leading to dramatically reduced response times.
- **Columnar Storage**: Consistent with modern lakehouse architectures, columnar storage formats can provide efficient data compression and swift retrieval for analytical queries requiring specific columns to be returned.

How to Plan for Real-Time Analytics

While preparing for real-time analytics, start by determining the criticality of real-time insights. Is immediate data crucial for decision-making, or would periodically updated insights suffice?

Remember that the costs associated with implementation can escalate when striving for real-time data. In many situations, a simpler micro-batch processing strategy could deliver substantial benefits without necessitating a complex or costly real-time architecture.

However, a real-time analytics database could be a fitting solution if operations involve high volumes of continually updated data (also known as data velocity)—such as in the financial services, fraud detection, e-commerce, or social media sectors.

Before proceeding, invest considerable time upskilling the team to understand the intricacies of event-driven architectures. This will ensure the organization possesses the requisite expertise and resources to support a real-time database platform.

Lastly, collaborate closely with potential vendor teams on small pilot programs before undertaking full-scale implementation—assess their suitability for specific needs. While some vendors offer schema-less SQL analytics, others focus on providing complex analytical data applications that integrate seamlessly with a data stack. Yet others may specialize in delivering the fastest response times in this category.

By executing well-structured proof-of-value projects early on, significant sums can be saved later in the project lifecycle. This approach also effectively communicates the benefits of real-time analytics databases to senior stakeholders at each delivery stage.

Instant Impact: Revolutionizing Insurance Pricing with Real-Time Analytics[10]

A large European insurance group aimed to deliver real-time pricing for its insurance products by incorporating over 800 factors for precise, bespoke customer quotations. Updating these rating factors in pricing models was traditionally lengthy, often taking weeks.

Using the real-time analytics database platform **Rockset** significantly boosted the customer's ability to adjust pricing models quickly. It improved the models' overall accuracy by incorporating new risk factors.

Processing Real-Time Streams

This chapter concludes with a discussion on stream processing, a method that enables real-time processing and insight generation from a continuous data flow. Stream processing is a critical element in the Modern Data Stack for businesses, especially those involved in real-time analytics, anomaly detection, and online ML.

Though present in various forms since the 1970s, stream processing gained momentum with the Internet's rise and the subsequent surge in data volume and velocity. The advent of Hadoop and MapReduce in the early 2000s saw companies like Google and Yahoo developing systems to process data streams in parallel with their distributed batch tools, giving birth to early stream processing systems like **Apache Storm** and **Apache Samza**.

Apache Flink, Spark Streaming, and Databricks Structured Streaming emerged in the mid-to-late 2010s, providing more powerful techniques for stream processing, like:

- **Event-Time Processing**: Handling data based on when events occur, rather than when they are processed.
- **Windowing:** Splitting a continuous data stream into discrete chunks to calculate metrics over the last five minutes, last hour, last day, etc.
- **Exactly-Once Processing**: Used to guarantee that each record in a data stream is processed only once and to effectively eliminate the risk of duplicate processing in the event of failure.

Once a stream processing system has processed an event, it's often not revisited. However, many streaming systems support reprocessing of historical data (for example, if the processing logic changes and there is a desire to recompute results). They also often have mechanisms to deal with late-arriving data (events that arrive after their window of relevance has passed).

A robust stream processing strategy can unlock real-time insights, offering businesses a competitive edge. The chosen stream processing solution must align with the use case. For instance,

Apache Flink excels at more complex processing logic, while Databricks Structured Streaming may be better suited to processing large volumes of data.

Ensure a strategy fulfills the functional requirements regarding latency and integrates seamlessly with the rest of the data stack so that real-time insights reach their intended users.

Consider nonfunctional requirements around ease of use for data engineering teams and end-users. Some platforms offer more user-friendly interfaces for building and managing real-time data pipelines compared to others, though this may require more code.

Lastly, monitoring and optimizing stream processing workloads is vital due to the mission-critical nature of real-time data analytics. Regularly fine-tune the data processing logic or scale resources to meet the necessary service levels.

Practical Advice and Next Steps

A lot of ground has been covered in this chapter. Still, there are several key takeaways around the importance of centralized storage and processing systems in the Modern Data Stack:

- Understand the evolution of capabilities offered by the traditional data warehouse, data lake, and the more recent data lakehouse.
- Consider the role of real-time data and its application to instant decision-making and improved customer experience in business processes.
- A cloud-based data strategy must consider business needs, data integration, geographical dispersion (including privacy and portability risks), and the pricing models of cloud service providers.
- Pay close attention to legacy data architectures. Understand the transition from on-premises to cloud-based data services.
- Know the concept of data gravity and understand its vital implications for data migration and the warehousing plan.
- Make data governance an early priority. With increas-

ing data volumes and varieties, it is vital to have a robust, adaptable data governance plan that includes data publication, access, usage, and quality assurance controls.
- The performance of benchmark tests specific to use cases might be beneficial, as opposed to relying on vendor-sponsored results if evaluating whether to use a specific vendor (e.g., Databricks or Snowflake).
- Experiment with DSML & AI tools and assess how they can integrate with existing workflows without requiring expensive data movement using commercial or open-source technologies.

Summary

This chapter provided a comprehensive look into the heart of the Modern Data Stack, covering technologies and architectures for data storage, querying, and processing for analysis.

The migration of data warehouses from on-premises systems to the cloud was explored, and strategic considerations for implementing a data warehouse in this context were covered.

Focus then shifted to the emergence of data lakes as a revolutionary storage and processing approach. In this context, distributed data processing tools like Apache Spark and the common pitfalls leading to the failure of data lakes—such as poor governance, subpar data quality, and inconsistent data formats—were discussed.

The evolution and convergence of these architectures, which led to the rise of the "data lakehouse"—a solution combining the scalability of data lakes and the performance of data warehouses—was also reviewed.

The chapter also emphasized incorporating data science and machine learning (DSML) into the Modern Data Stack. This involves choosing appropriate frameworks based on the type of problem, ease of use, community support, and long-term team competency development.

Moreover, how vendor (and open-source) technology continually evolves to support real-time data querying and processing—catering to business needs for timely insights from fast-moving data sources and ultra-low latency requirements—was also reviewed.

The exploration of data storage, querying, and processing underscored a crucial point: raw data often needs further refinement to harness its full potential. This is where data transformation is critical, transforming raw data into accessible, understandable, and actionable insights.

In the following chapter, this transformation stage is examined in more detail. It is a critical component that shapes the data into an actionable and understandable form for end-users.

Chapter 4 References

[1] Rodero, José, José Toval, and Mario Piattini. "The Audit of the Data Warehouse Framework." July 1999. https://ceur-ws. org/Vol-19/paper14.pdf.

[2] "Dimensional Modeling Techniques." Kimball Group. Accessed August 28, 2023. https://www.kimballgroup.com/ data-warehouse-business-intelligence-resources/kimball-techniques/dimensional-modeling-techniques/.

[3] Goretsky, Rob. "MLB Moves to BigQuery Data Warehouse." Google Cloud Blog. August 11, 2020. https://cloud.google. com/blog/products/data-analytics/mlb-moves-to-bigquery-data-warehouse.

[4] "Customer Story: ABN AMRO." Databricks. Accessed August 13, 2023. https://www.databricks.com/customers/abn-amro.

[5] Grattarola, Florencia. "Rina Dechter: Deep Learning Pioneer." A Computer of One's Own. December 15, 2018. https:// medium.com/a-computer-of-ones-own/rina-dechter-deep-learning-pioneer-e7e9ccc96c6e.

[6] Wikipedia. "Deep Learning." Last modified May 10, 2019. https://en.wikipedia.org/ wiki/Deep_learning.

7 "Browse the State-of-The-Art in Machine Learning." Papers With Code. Accessed August 28, 2023. https://paperswithcode.com/sota.

8 Goodfellow, Ian J., et al. "Generative Adversarial Networks." arXiv:1406.2661. June 10, 2014. https://arxiv.org/abs/1406.2661.

9 Vaswani, Ashish, et al. "Attention Is All You Need." arXiv:1706.03762. June 12, 2017. https://arxiv.org/abs/1706.03762.

10 "Allianz Direct Advances Digital Insurance Innovation with Real-Time Pricing Powered by Rockset." Rockset. December 20, 2022. https://rockset.com/press/allianz-direct-real-time-pricing-powered-by-rockset/.

Chapter 5

Reshaping and Redefining Data

The significance of data transformation in today's information-driven world has skyrocketed, echoing the broader evolution of the Modern Data Stack. Organizations now grapple with an unprecedented volume of data collected from disparate sources, often presented in various formats and marred by inconsistencies or duplication.

Data transformation serves as the remedy to these challenges, reshaping data into formats that lend themselves to analytics and paving the way for precise and actionable insights. In the broader context of extract, transform, load (ETL) or extract, load, transform (ELT) processes, data transformation represents the critical "T" that enables successful data ingestion, transportation, and processing.

The transformation process entails extracting data from many source systems, tailoring it to fit operational and analytics requirements, and subsequently loading it into a target environment or system. Beyond this core use case, transformation platforms serve a broader role in preparing an organization's data for various end-user scenarios discussed in Chapter 6, ranging from conventional business intelligence and reporting to collaborative data applications, AI, and beyond.

The evolution of data transformation technology has mirrored the broader changes in the data landscape. In the early days of business computing, data transformation was a predominantly manual, code-intensive process, but in the late 1990s and early 2000s ETL tools like IBM's **DataStage**, **Informatica**, Microsoft's **SQL Server Integration Services (SSIS)**, and Cognos **Decision-Stream** began to streamline and automate the process.

The mid-to-late 2010s saw the rise of a new generation of ETL tools like **Alteryx**, **Trifacta** (acquired by Alteryx), **Talend** (acquired by Qlik), and Matillion that worked in tandem with the surge in cloud technologies and the drive towards democratized analytics. These platforms offered advanced data transformation and modeling capabilities like data cleansing, normalization, aggregation, and wider integration with analytics tools, often in a visual, code-free, or low-code environment.

Data transformation has assumed a pivotal role in the Modern Data Stack. Technologies like dbt (data build tool) are revolutionizing data transformation, offering a toolkit for executing complex transformations using standard SQL, thus enabling robust data modeling and presentation for a growing audience of data-savvy stakeholders.

Maintaining clarity and consistency for business users becomes a significant challenge in the face of increasingly complex data architectures. Users are often presented with reports, dashboards, collaborative notebooks, or analytic applications, each claiming to offer a single version of the truth. However, each separate analytics tool usually defines its own key metrics and business terms, which leads to inconsistencies.

Historically, these were managed by individual vendors through unique *semantic layers*: logical mappings between the physical data stored in the technology stack, along with business terminology. Today, these traditional BI layers are evolving into modern metrics layers and integrated platforms designed to mitigate the chaos of working with data from multiple sources.

In this chapter, the nuances of data transformation will be explored more deeply, touching on its role in the ETL process, how it shapes modern data modeling practices, and how contemporary tools are adapting to fit into the framework of the Modern Data Stack.

Figure 5.1: High-Level Data Transformation Functions for the Modern Data Stack

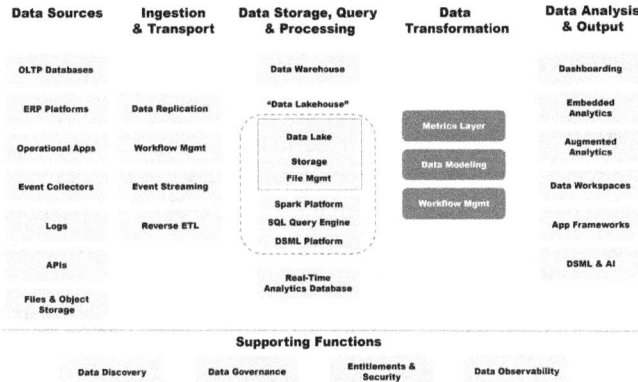

Data Sources	Ingestion & Transport	Data Storage, Query & Processing	Data Transformation	Data Analysis & Output
OLTP Databases		Data Warehouse		Dashboarding
ERP Platforms	Data Replication	"Data Lakehouse"	Metrics Layer	Embedded Analytics
Operational Apps	Workflow Mgmt	Data Lake	Data Modeling	Augmented Analytics
		Storage		
		File Mgmt		
Event Collectors	Event Streaming	Spark Platform	Workflow Mgmt	Data Workspaces
Logs	Reverse ETL	SQL Query Engine		App Frameworks
		DSML Platform		
APIs		Real-Time Analytics Database		DSML & AI
Files & Object Storage				

Supporting Functions

Data Discovery	Data Governance	Entitlements & Security	Data Observability

Building a Data Transformation and Modeling Strategy

Given the multitude of data sources under consideration, building out a robust data modeling strategy becomes essential to manage the incoming information deluge.

Different data consumers will likely have varying expectations and needs regarding their data. Consequently, a one-size-fits-all approach may need to be revised to address such diverse requirements. A more pragmatic solution might lie in a hybrid strategy that balances costs, delivery timelines, and user satisfaction, which potentially provides a more effective solution than rigid adherence to a singular data-modeling approach.

Particularly in the context of cloud computing, processing of data is often the costliest component, superseding storage. However, many existing data modeling patterns originated when storage was considerably more expensive.

Therefore, while best practices from two decades ago may still hold relevance if they generate explicit data models that help execute a coherent data strategy, it's essential to maintain a critical perspective. Challenge the status quo, and don't shy away from questioning and revising outdated norms.

Common Approaches to Data Modeling

The analytical data landscape today predominantly uses four main patterns of data modeling.

Normalized Modeling

As discussed in previous chapters, source systems such as ERPs might consist of thousands of meticulously defined transactional tables. A Corporate Information Factory (CIF), attributed to Bill Inmon and Claudia Imhoff, mirrors this complexity, necessitating substantial data joins (i.e., combinations) to arrive at the final analytical result.[1]

To provide more accessible structures to end-users, Inmon suggested the creation of data marts derived from this centralized data warehouse. Data marts might exist separately for finance, marketing, sales, and so on, designed to cater to the specific needs of business units or departments within an organization.

The data within these marts undergoes denormalization or restructuring into a dimensional model (like a star schema or a snowflake schema). This process optimizes the readability and performance of the data based on the particular business unit's needs. As a result, denormalization simplifies the task for business users when querying the data or generating reports.

Figure 5.2: Inmon Corporate Information Factory (CIF) Architecture[2]

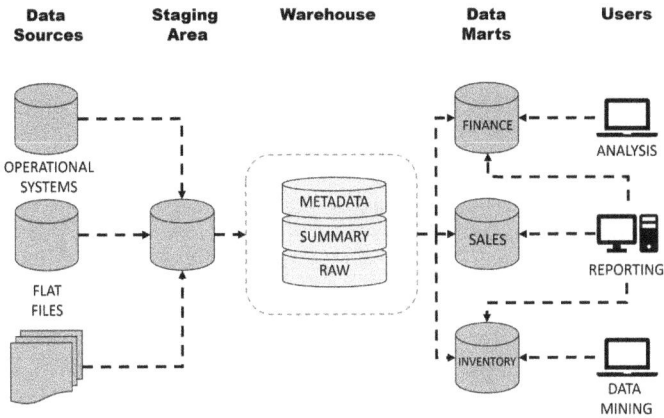

Dimensional (Denormalized) Modeling

Another widely employed approach to data modeling for analytics is dimensional modeling, also known as the Kimball Method. The brainchild of Ralph Kimball, Margy Ross, and other data warehousing experts in the 1990s, this method was defined by its bottom-up approach, as opposed to Inmon's top-down CIF.[3]

The Kimball Method centers around a "star schema" in which dimension tables surround a central fact table. The fact table holds the measurable, quantitative data (facts), while the dimension tables contain descriptive attributes related to the facts.

Owing to its simplicity, the star schema design is more intuitive and straightforward for end-users to comprehend and navigate. This clarity also simplifies writing queries and generating reports while presenting a structure optimized for performance through indexing and partitioning.

A star schema generally models a distinct business process at its most granular, transactional level. However, aggregated star schemas are possible, although they come with the compromise of sacrificing detail for improved performance.

Kimball also introduced the notion of conformed dimensions, which maintain consistency across different star schemas.

Conformed dimensions enable cross-functional analysis and reporting, eliminating the need for the intensive up-front modeling efforts demanded by the CIF approach.

Figure 5.3: **Example of a Denormalized Star Schema Model**[4]

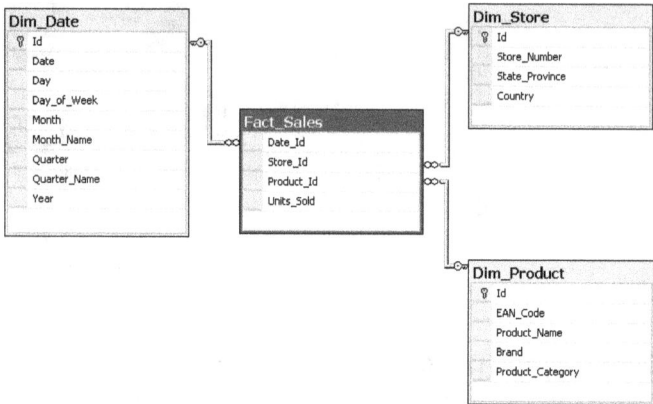

Data Vault Modeling

The data vault modeling approach has been gaining traction since the 2010s and is favored for its flexibility, scalability, and adaptability.[5]

The model consists of three main components that allow the data vault model to handle complex, interconnected datasets efficiently:

- **Hubs**: Representing business keys or identifiers.
- **Links**: Defining relationships between data elements.
- **Satellites**: Representing descriptive attributes of data.

The data vault model shines because of its agility and scalability and its design to accommodate swift changes in business requirements. This makes it a fitting choice for dynamic, fast-paced scenarios that deal with large and diverse volumes of data. It also excels in data models that incorporate information from various systems by maintaining the representation of the source system's data and facilitating easier ongoing integration of new sources.

A vital characteristic of the data vault model is its strong emphasis on maintaining a history of data changes. It preserves all data, even if received in a damaged or incorrect format. This capability allows for complete traceability and auditability, which can be crucial for nonfunctional requirements like use cases involving heavy regulation or compliance.

Despite its unique advantages, the data vault model has potential downsides. It can be challenging to understand and implement compared to Kimball's dimensional models. The model's deliberate focus on flexibility and adaptability comes at the cost of slower query performance. Many practitioners include additional business-facing layers (such as data marts) to counterbalance this and enhance reporting and analysis efficiency.

Figure 5.4: A Simple Data Vault Model with Two Hubs, One Link, and Four Satellites[6]

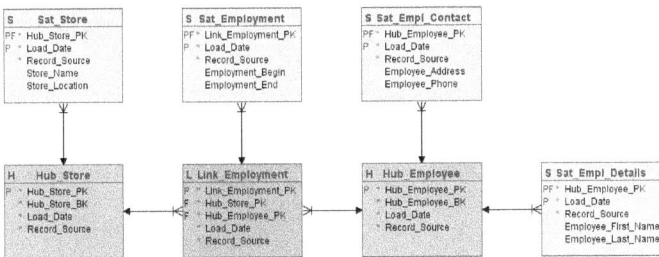

One Big Table (OBT) Modeling

One big table (OBT) is a newer approach that involves the creation of expansive denormalized models. This method offers the advantage of speed and ease in initial setup, but it could lead to high computational costs and data redundancy.

In the Modern Data Stack context—where storage costs are a fraction of compute costs—the main argument for OBT lies in its cost-effectiveness, performance, and shorter implementation time.[7] Evidence suggests that wide tables are 25–50 percent faster than star schema queries, primarily because they eliminate the need for joins.

However, the OBT approach comes with its own set of challenges. The "one big table" can quickly evolve into "hundreds of big tables," leading to data duplication and inconsistency due to the isolated creation of data models across different teams.

As such, it's vital to implement design patterns like columnar storage and compression to prevent data redundancy from affecting query performance. Additionally, it's crucial to consider scalability plans early in the design process, as managing a single large table can become increasingly complex over time.

As with most architecture decisions in the Modern Data Stack, the "one-size-fits-all" approach rarely yields better results. Hybrid strategies often provide more effective solutions, like integrating wide data marts from the OBT approach with the structured modeling from star schema best practices.

The dynamics and responsibilities of the team involved in the modeling decision should also be considered. For instance, data engineers and architects could be tasked with data modeling, while analytics engineers or analysts could focus on consumer-facing data marts and end-user analytics.

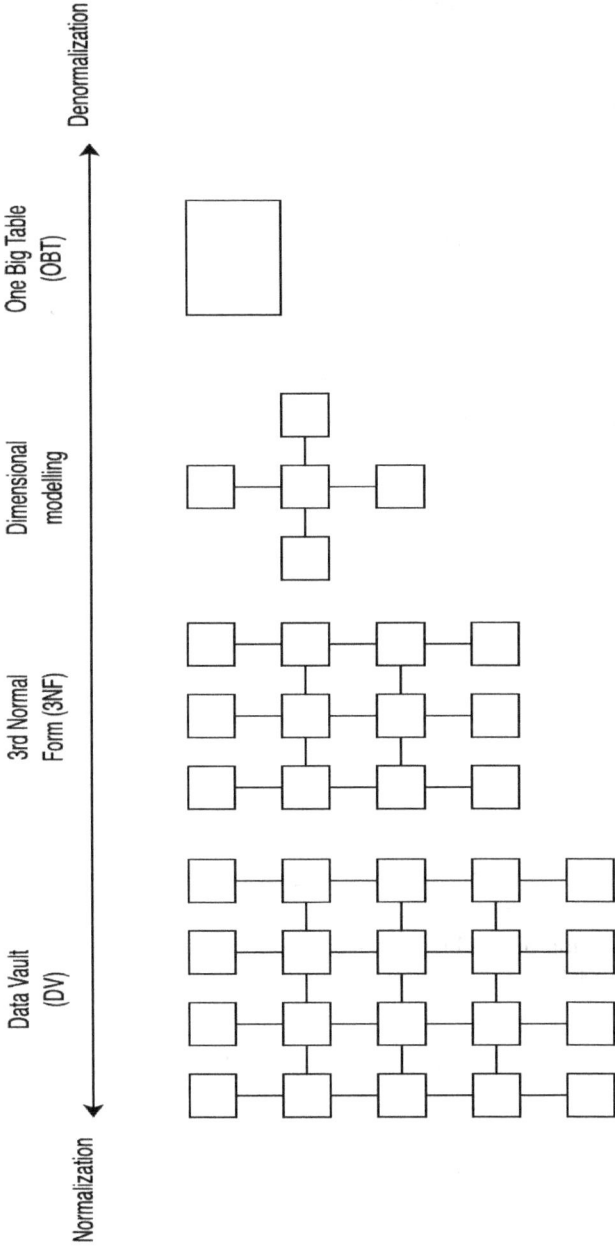

Figure 5.5: Comparison between Modeling Techniques Described in This Chapter[8]

Normalization

Denormalization

Data Vault (DV)

3rd Normal Form (3NF)

Dimensional modelling

One Big Table (OBT)

Bridging the Gap Between Data Model to Data Engineering

Considering these team dynamics, data modeling can be approached from either the engineering or the analyst perspective. The Modern Data Stack offers a variety of platforms and technologies depending on the route chosen.

From an engineering perspective, data modeling needs to serve a specific purpose. The teams coding and releasing small, modular, and incremental changes will require a modeling solution that integrates seamlessly with version control environments. This enables continuous integration and continuous deployment (CI/CD), allowing for automated data quality tests and code consistency through style guides.

dbt in Focus

Developed by **Fishtown Analytics** in 2016, the open-source product dbt (data build tool) was designed to meet these engineering requirements. It has since seen a meteoric rise in popularity, forming strategic alliances with major vendors like Snowflake, Databricks, and others. As of this writing, the enterprise version, **dbt Cloud Enterprise**, boasts several thousand customers.

dbt plays a crucial role in the "transform" phase (a concept covered throughout this book) of the ELT process. It allows users to execute transformations directly in SQL, enabling analytics engineers to model data through standard, repeatable methods. However, it's essential to note that dbt doesn't handle data extraction or loading; it focuses solely on transformation and data modeling.

The tool consists of three main components:

- **Development**: Where users craft transformations in SQL and implement business logic.
- **Testing**: Where users conduct tests to ensure the transformed data is formatted correctly.

- **Documentation**: Where documentation for the transformations is produced.

Its ability to create modular code—reusable SQL snippets deployable across various transformations and projects is where dbt really shines. This feature significantly reduces the volume of code needed to construct and maintain a data transformation pipeline.

The modern, designer-friendly Python templating language **Jinja** is what dbt leverages to build these reusable components ("macros"). Macros can take arguments to customize the underlying SQL code, as is done with functions in programming languages or functional blocks in everyday tools like **Microsoft Excel**.

Jinja templating allows for the embedding of logic into SQL code using Jinja syntax, thus introducing programming concepts like *for-loops* or *if-then-else* statements into regular SQL code. This feature proves particularly useful when dynamically generating SQL code based on certain conditions or iterating over a list of values.

Each transformation in dbt is defined in a distinct SQL file known as a *model*. Models can reference other models, enabling engineers to construct intricate transformations by piecing together smaller steps into a complete workflow. This structure promotes modularity in transformation code, making it easier to understand and maintain.

As engineers prepare their code for the complete analytics lifecycle, dbt provides extensive configuration for the models, ensuring that development code targets suitable environments and that test and production data are used only when appropriate. This approach promotes robust controls and data governance throughout the engineering process, mitigating risks of data leakage or other adverse impacts.

A Publisher's Journey to Enhanced Collaboration[9]

A multimedia publishing giant had accumulated a complex legacy architecture with data residing in multiple siloed sources.

To simplify data architecture and increase collaboration, the company implemented Databricks Lakehouse and dbt Cloud to build reusable data ingestion frameworks for significant data sources and rapid data modeling for analytics, ML, and reporting.

Once launched, the team quickly had 85 dbt models across various domains, which led to a 30 percent increase in self-service among data warehousing engineers (saving 16 hours per data integration sprint). The company also improved data integrity and trust among business users, mainly through dbt tests at various data points.

Don't Write Off Traditional ETL Tools (Yet)

Of course, dbt isn't the only game in town, no matter what the Modern Data Stack venture capital (VC)-backed hype might suggest.

Traditional ETL tools have long provided comparable functionality. Current offerings include low-code visual workflows with version control and other features that are just as impressive as those found in dbt.

Options for managed transformation services from vendors such as Matillion, Informatica, and Trifacta (now incorporated into the Alteryx cloud platform) can simplify the administration of larger enterprise transformation workflows. However, remember that these advantages may come with a higher price tag than pure open-source alternatives.

Embracing Data Literacy with Analyst-Friendly Tools

Beyond data engineers, there's excellent value in democratizing governed access to data and models for the broad audience of business and data analysts across an organization, and not just the technical specialists. However, merely providing access to data isn't sufficient; data literacy also requires individuals can effectively read, work with, analyze, and communicate using data.

Prominent industry figures like Jordan Morrow, author of *Be Data Literate*, advocate incorporating data literacy as a fundamental aspect of an organization's culture.[10] Data literacy, as an organizational concept, transcends mere comprehension of data. It includes asking the right questions, making data-driven decisions, and communicating effectively with data.

Becoming data literate often involves engaging with the raw data and understanding how that data is shaped, represented, and shared across a business. While some data analysts may still grapple with preparing data in tools like Microsoft Excel, others have adopted self-service analytics tools like **Alteryx Designer**, **Tableau Prep**, **Prophecy,** or **Savant**. These tools allow end-users to prepare, blend, and analyze data using no-code, repeatable workflows.

Self-service tools aim to simplify data transformation and modeling processes, making the data more consistent and user-friendly for analytics consumption (a topic of the next chapter). These tools might offer drag-and-drop features that allow users to prepare and blend data from various sources, including Excel, SQL databases, cloud sources, or APIs.

Many self-service platforms include statistical, predictive, prescriptive, or spatial analytics tools. These features empower business users to execute complex advanced analytics without the need to write code or depend on the expertise of external teams.

Looker and LookML

Emerging in the early 2010s as a part of the **Looker** data platform, **LookML** has been a critical component in the past decade's data modeling revolution. Following Looker's acquisition by Google Cloud in 2020, it and its LookML language have been integrated into Google Cloud's suite of data management and BI solutions.

Rather than a SQL replacement, LookML is a language that describes business attributes, aggregates, calculations, and data relationships in a SQL database. Situated as a layer on top of SQL, it empowers data analysts to construct models and establish consistent analytics across the organization. It leverages definitions provided in the LookML model to abstract and generate SQL.

In LookML, data models encompass *explores* (significant entities in the data, such as users and orders), *views* (specific perspectives on the data, generally corresponding to a SQL table or derived table), and *fields* (columns in a view). Each of these objects is configured with specific parameters that clarify the object's behavior and characteristics.

LookML boasts a range of functionalities, including derived tables, table calculations, filtered measures, dimensions, HTML drill links, and more. It targets a mixed audience of data analysts and engineers familiar with SQL within the Modern Data Stack. This is a departure from tools like Alteryx, Savant, or Tableau Prep, which don't require coding skills.

These platforms generally offer the concept of repeatable workflows similar to dbt's models and templates, meaning that they can be saved, shared, and reused. This helps ensure consistent results and improves productivity for business units, which are often heavily time-constrained when running daily or weekly tasks exclusively in messy or inconsistent spreadsheets.

Enriching Transactional Data with Geospatial Analytics for Strategic Insights[11]

A leading online restaurant delivery service uses data to improve its service. It launched a new program that enriches transactional data with geospatial analytics to understand the demand for delivery-only restaurants in cities across Europe.

They used LookML, the modeling language of Looker, to define metrics (like conversion rate) once, and then users were given the autonomy to create their reports and dashboards using these central definitions. This relieved the BI team from the burden of writing one-off queries, allowing analysts to be more strategic.

Analytic Automation

The notion of repeatability in transformation and modeling naturally leads to a critical question: How can it be guaranteed that transformation workflows or models are effectively refreshed on demand or at a set frequency?

For projects focused on data engineering, workflow orchestration tools like Apache Airflow, **Luigi**, or **Prefect** are instrumental in managing intricate workflows and schedules. These tools employ visual workflows that consist of tasks executed in a specified order and triggered by set schedules or specific events.

Workflows can be merged, divided, or run concurrently as necessary. Workflow orchestration tools typically offer advanced monitoring and debugging views, showcasing running status, completed tasks, and detailed logging information. Workflows can be manually initiated, halted, or retried in case of failure, and any anomalies, failures, or significant data changes will trigger alerts to notify the relevant team or individual.

For analyst-facing tools, vendors commonly provide automation directly within the user platform (such as the cloud-hosted service by Savant) or as an additional architectural component (like **Alteryx Server** or **Tableau Prep Conductor**).

Transformation or modeling workflows are developed on an analyst's local machine and then submitted for execution against production data using a remote server. This server incorporates version control, roll-back, and data governance policies.

The Metrics Layer: Take Control or Lose It?

Successful implementation of transformation and modeling within a data stack means that carefully curated and well-defined data can seamlessly flow into end-user environments such as business intelligence tools, dashboards, analyst workbenches, and data science platforms.

As an organization's analytics maturity evolves, projects that initially began as ad hoc, one-off questions transition into more structured processes subject to robust governance and automation controls. This standardization process mitigates much of the initial chaos and excitement surrounding using new data for generating insights.

However, the journey to building analytic utilities is often fraught with challenges. One such challenge is the risk of inconsistency and duplication when various teams use analytics to answer business questions, potentially overlapping use cases or problem areas.

Consider a situation where a business uses a metric like annual recurring revenue (ARR) to evaluate sales performance. Different teams could calculate ARR uniquely without a centrally stored and agreed-upon definition, leading to inconsistent results and potential disputes reminiscent of previous decades' infamous "dueling spreadsheets" scenarios.

The concept of a metrics layer has been introduced to the Modern Data Stack to address this issue. As a centralized repository for key business metrics, this layer bridges an organization's processing and transformation layers and downstream analytics tools. It connects to various tools—ranging from CRM suites, BI tools, and in-house tools—to data quality and experimentation tools.

A metrics layer allows data teams to define and store business-friendly metrics or key performance indicators in code, typically SQL or Python. This single repository for business metrics ensures consistent metric logic across all analytical tasks.

In our example, ARR gets defined once in the metrics layer. That definition becomes available in various technologies, such as Tableau, PowerBI, Dataiku, or analytic applications written with Python.

Large enterprise tech companies pioneered these tools, often due to frustration with the challenges of governance and the expanding variety of internal data consumption points. Airbnb built **Minerva**, Uber created **uMetric**, and LinkedIn developed their **Unified Metrics Platform**, each serving as the organization's internal single source of truth for all business metrics.

An integrated metrics layer centralizes key business data definitions and improves data teams' efficiency by eliminating the need for repeated analytics. This fosters a culture of data-driven decision-making and democratization across the organization, with data stakeholders becoming the key owners of these metrics.

Moreover, a metrics layer enhances transparency between technical and nontechnical teams by providing a unified interface for metrics information. This consistency in understanding and interpreting key metrics allows all teams to speak the same language, regardless of the tools they use to compute the metrics.

The metrics layer also simplifies the tracking of changes as businesses evolve and alter their metrics' definitions. For instance, when ASC 606 was introduced as a new revenue recognition standard, financial planning and analysis (FP&A) teams across various companies grappled with the rule's complexity and implications for dashboards, reports, and regulatory submissions.

A metrics layer provided stakeholders with alerts anytime the lineage or definition of a metric changes, enabling them to make sense of data, especially when a new metric definition led to abnormal or unexpected results.

The metrics layer could revolutionize how data is consumed within organizations and traditional BI's role in this process.

However, it's still early days for technologies aiming to realize this potential. Vendors like **GoodData** and **cube.dev** have had success adapting their innovative platforms to make "headless BI"[12] or "data-as-a-service" (DaaS) as terms to watch in this fast-moving space.

Practical Advice and Next Steps

- Understand that one-size-fits-all solutions are unlikely to cater to all scenarios and a business's need for data transformation and modeling.
- Be ready to question and challenge any *quasi-religious* modeling viewpoints of data architects that misalign with project budgets, timelines, or performance expectations.
- Provide clear, consistent data for business users, which is essential in the face of complex data architectures and pipelines. In the past, in isolation, vendors have managed these through their tools. Still, modern metrics layers seek to provide universally accepted data definitions across a wide range of analyst tools.
- Explore user appetite for low-code or no-code data transformation capabilities to complement more advanced data engineering toolsets. Consider the costs and opportunities platforms like dbt provide to enable complex modular transformations using standard SQL.
- Remember, data transformation aims to reshape raw data into a more valuable and practical format for decision-making, insights, and predictive analytics. It's crucial to continually revisit and refine the data transformation strategy as business needs and technologies evolve.

Summary

Throughout this chapter, the integral role of data transformation and modeling within the Modern Data Stack has been explored. First by addressing the fundamental task of rectifying inconsistency or redundancy, then moving to the enabling of more complex analytics (a subject to be covered more deeply in the next chapter).

The evolution of data transformation and modeling—from its coding-heavy inception to the rise of more straightforward, user-friendly visual ETL tools—was traced. How the advent of self-service analytics and cloud computing, spearheaded by platforms like Alteryx, Trifacta, and Talend, was highlighted. This has democratized data transformation, making it more accessible and adaptable for business users.

The growing popularity of platforms such as dbt (data build tool) attests to the changing landscape of data transformation, indicating the increasing demand for more sophisticated, accessible tools that democratize data processing.

However, it's crucial to recognize the challenges these tools bring. Consistency across different tools and interpretations can be a considerable concern, mainly when dealing with intricate data architectures and diverse data sources.

In such scenarios, modern metrics layers and integrated platforms are indispensable. These solutions offer a way to standardize and simplify defining and comprehending key metrics and business terms.

Lastly, the chapter addressed the importance of ensuring repeatability and the successful refreshing of workflows—a critical step to guaranteeing that transformed and modeled data reaches its intended endpoints.

Be it analyst tools, analytic applications, or data science platforms, all these components rely on meticulously curated data to generate insights and value by solidifying the architecture of our Modern Data Stack.

Chapter 5 References

1 "Corporate Information Factory." ScienceDirect. Accessed August 28, 2023. https://www.sciencedirect.com/topics/computer-science/corporate-information-factory.

2 Image courtesy of "Oracle9i Data Warehousing Guide:

Release 2 (9.2)." https://docs.oracle.com/cd/B10501_01/
server.920/a96520/concept.htm.

[3] "Dimensional Modeling Techniques." Kimball Group. Accessed August 28, 2023. https://www.kimballgroup.com/ data-warehouse-business-intelligence-resources/kimball-techniques/dimensional-modeling-techniques/.

[4] "Dimensional Data Modeling." LearnDataModeling.com. Accessed August 28, 2023. https://learndatamodeling. com/blog/dimensional-data-modeling/. Image courtesy of Wikipedia. "Star Schema." August 16, 2023. https:// en.wikipedia.org/wiki/Star_schema.

[5] "What Is a Data Vault?" Databricks. Accessed August 28, 2023. https://www.databricks.com/ glossary/data-vault.

[6] Wikipedia. "Data Vault Modeling." Last modified January 31, 2021. https://en.wikipedia.org/ wiki/Data_Vault_Modeling [including image].

[7] Kaminsky, Michael. "Star Schema vs. OBT for Data Warehouse Performance." Fivetran. August 16, 2022. https:// www.fivetran.com/blog/star-schema-vs-obt.

[8] Neo, Jonathan. "Building a Kimball Dimensional Model with Dbt." dbt. April 20, 2023. https://docs.getdbt.com/blog/ kimball-dimensional-model.

[9] "Condé Nast Serves up Multimedia Content on a Global Scale." dbt. Accessed August 28, 2023. https://www.getdbt. com/success-stories/cond%C3%A9-nast/.

[10] Morrow, Jordan. *Be Data Literate: The Data Literacy Skills Everyone Needs to Succeed*. London: Kogan Page, 2021.

[11] "Deliveroo: A Customer Story Deliveroo Uses Looker to Transport Delicious Meals Faster." Looker. n.d. https://media. bitpipe.com/io_14x/io_143297/item_1732776/deliveroo-case-study.pdf.

[12] Armstrong, Jarred. 2023. "Headless BI: A Flexible and Scalable Approach to Business Intelligence." LinkedIn. April 4, 2023. https://www.linkedin.com/pulse/headless-bi-flexible-scalable-approach-business-jarred-armstrong/.

Chapter 6

Analysis and Output in the Modern Data Stack

In earlier chapters, the Modern Data Stack's ingestion and transport of data into centralized cloud repositories for storage, query, and processing has been explained. And in the previous chapter, how this raw data is shaped and modeled to deliver clarity and consistency to business users around common business analytics terms in the form of metrics was discussed.

Now, it's time to focus on this data's consumption and delivery. The goal? To provide a conduit for actionable insights to users, subject matter experts, and decision-makers. So, in this chapter, the functions that enable analytics integration into business processes—to enhance top-line financials, mitigate costs, and foster a high-performing analytic culture through improved data literacy—are highlighted.

The essential capabilities for reporting and dashboarding (exploring their role as critical visual interfaces for data) and the direct embedding of analytic capabilities into operational applications (allowing for seamless data exploration and question-asking without users needing to switch tools, thereby bolstering efficiency) are touched upon.

The evolution of augmented analytics, particularly how recent advancements in genAI and NLP are revolutionizing data architectures while enhancing the user experience, is described. In addition, the rise of cloud-based analyst workbenches—and the new forms of collaboration they enable—will be delved into.

As businesses increasingly rely on sophisticated analytics to maintain a competitive edge, a deep dive into data science machine learning and artificial intelligence (DSML & AI) platforms—and how AI begins within our data stack— will take place. These platforms (and their components) support automating and simplifying the construction, deployment, and monitoring of ML models on a large scale.

Lastly, the emergence of analytic application frameworks will be evaluated. By enabling the creation and deployment of web-based applications, these frameworks offer novel ways for decision-makers to interact with and explore the data within the Modern Data Stack.

Figure 6.1: High-Level Functions for Data Analysis and Output

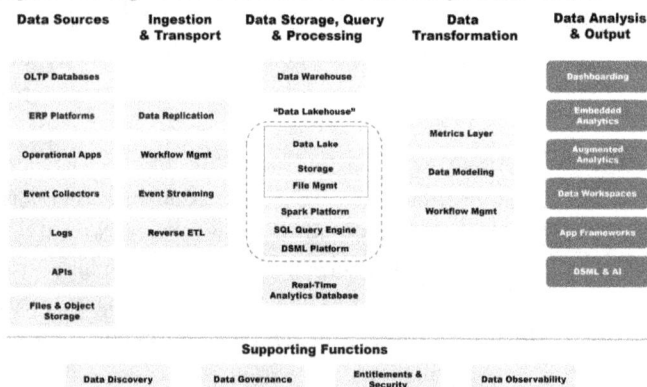

Data Sources	Ingestion & Transport	Data Storage, Query & Processing	Data Transformation	Data Analysis & Output
OLTP Databases		Data Warehouse		Dashboarding
ERP Platforms	Data Replication	"Data Lakehouse"		Embedded Analytics
Operational Apps	Workflow Mgmt	Data Lake	Metrics Layer	Augmented Analytics
Event Collectors	Event Streaming	Storage / File Mgmt	Data Modeling	Data Workspaces
Logs	Reverse ETL	Spark Platform / SQL Query Engine	Workflow Mgmt	App Frameworks
APIs		DSML Platform		DSML & AI
Files & Object Storage		Real-Time Analytics Database		

Supporting Functions

Data Discovery	Data Governance	Entitlements & Security	Data Observability

Business Intelligence and Dashboarding

Business intelligence, a cornerstone in contemporary decision-making processes, traces its roots back to the earliest days of industrial commerce and finance. In the 1860s, the term was first used by author Richard Millar Devens to describe how Sir Henry

Furnese, a banker, gained a competitive edge by gathering and acting on information before his competitors.[1]

The term was reinvented in the 1950s by IBM's Hans Peter Luhn to denote technologies that were automating these processes, including the advent of the hard disk drive, which vastly increased data storage capabilities.[2] However, only highly specialized individuals could transform raw data into actionable information during BI's early days.

Fast forward to the 1970s, when companies like SAP began developing BI for larger corporate clients, facilitating their data compilation into databases, and generating reports. Companies like **Nielsen** were early adopters of BI, using it to discern sales trends and retail analytics. The late 1970s and 1980s witnessed the widespread deployment of complex early-generation data warehouses, which demanded a dedicated IT staff to run reports.

Decision support systems (DSS), a precursor to modern BI, emerged around this time as businesses began recognizing the value of data-driven insights. Tools providing more straightforward ways to access and organize data surfaced, including online analytical processing (OLAP) and executive information systems (EIS), which pulled data from centralized data warehouses.

BI tooling for templated reporting, ad hoc analysis, and OLAP cube access became more commonplace in the late 1990s, although these solutions were often expensive and inflexible. Second-generation BI tools such as Qlik and Tableau emerged in the mid-2000s in response to the business need for flexible, easy-to-use visual solutions that were now possible due to the increases in processing power of desktop PCs and a shift from 32-bit to 64-bit PC architectures, which meant significantly more data could be analyzed in memory at high-speed.

The 2010s heralded the arrival of the first cloud BI software, interactive business dashboards, and self-service analytics software—moving decision-makers closer to data. While reporting has significantly advanced from the "green bar" reports of the recent past, there's still ongoing innovation in how reporting is executed in the Modern Data Stack.

A growing focus is on rendering complex data understandable for nontechnical users, which is realized through interactive dashboards, data storytelling, and real-time data interaction. Data storytelling melds data visualization best practices with narrative storytelling to simplify complex data presentation.

How to Develop a Strong Dashboard Strategy

An effective dashboard strategy starts with audience-centric design—listening to user needs and presenting information in simple, clear visuals. Recognizing that effective dashboard design is iterative and that analysts must refine their work based on user feedback and their subsequent evolving needs is a vital part of the process.

As with all data consumption aspects, the data that informs reports and dashboards must be of high quality and reflect known uncertainties. This requires well-documented data pipelines and traceable data lineage back to sources for accountability.

Lastly, ensuring users understand dashboard utilization and data interpretation is essential. Dashboards and reports need to be treated as data products produced by the organization and should be retired or reengineered if usage wanes, as opposed to persisting in the form of a "data swamp" (as was covered earlier).

> **Breaking the Backlog: Revolutionizing Quick-Commerce Analytics in the Cloud**[3]
>
> For an analytics provider specializing in quick-commerce retail, delivering high-quality reporting and insights to a growing customer base was challenging. It struggled to analyze large datasets and create custom visualizations for the many brands in its customer base. Reliant on Excel and PowerPoint while preparing and blending multiple data extracts led to a lengthy reporting cycle and frequent backlogs.
>
> The company turned to **Sigma**, a cloud-based data analytics solution that integrates with Snowflake Data Sharing, which enabled secure, fast transformation and delivery of

large datasets. The customer developed customizable, automatic dashboards for their main clients, which were updated continuously in granular detail, allowing clients to answer their ad hoc questions without requiring assistance from the central analytics team.

This implementation led to a 90 percent reduction in data delivery turnaround time, from 2–3 weeks to 2–3 days, and a 200 percent increase in capacity without additional personnel. The company could focus on offering higher-quality data to its clients with deeper self-service analytics.

The Death of the Dashboard?

In recent years, an increasing chorus of industry voices has pointed out the limitations of traditional dashboards.[4,5] Critics argue that they haven't kept up with the exponential increase in data volumes, data formats (text, images, audio, etc.), or the imperative for real-time decision-making insights.

This deficiency was glaringly obvious during the COVID-19 pandemic when organizations had to dramatically adjust their operating models in response to rapidly changing customer behaviors.

Detractors argue that dashboards have evolved into static, high-maintenance displays of increasingly complex data, providing little value to average business users. This ineffectiveness has led to inefficient deployments and disappointing returns on investment.

In response to poorly designed and implemented dashboards, investments in the Modern Data Stack are shifting away from isolated dashboards and static reports. Instead, the focus is now on embedding real-time insights directly into operational systems. By leveraging the power of AI and ML, decision-making capabilities are being integrated into the systems people use daily, bringing data closer to action.

For instance, in the retail sector, instead of relying on traditional dashboards for inventory management, real-time data embedded within their operational systems allows businesses to respond swiftly to changes in demand patterns. This dynamic and immediate approach represents a significant shift in data usage, ultimately enabling more agile, informed decision-making.

Extending the Reach with Embedded Analytics

In 2017, Gartner analysts Cindi Howson and Rita Sallam pointed out that "Pervasive business intelligence remains elusive, with BI and analytics adoption at about 30% of all employees. Data and analytics leaders wanting to extend the reach and impact of BI and analytics in their organizations should deploy modern BI platforms, leveraging mobile and embedding capabilities."[6]

This perspective underscores the importance of embedded analytics—a category of delivery that directly integrates data analytics capabilities, such as reporting and dashboarding, into business applications or websites.

Embedded analytics allow users to gain relevant insights within the context of their regular workflows, eliminating the need to switch between systems or lose their train of thought. For instance, a sales team might embed an analytics feed into a CRM system or internal tool, ensuring all their latest metrics can be found in one place.

Application programming interfaces (APIs) that enable apps to interact and integrate with third-party components are relied on for embedded analytics. These integrations manage how BI content—like data sources, dashboards, and reports—are embedded, customized, and automated, and how they interact with each other. Therefore, effective API management—which includes optimizing traffic, user authentication, security, and compliance—is vital for delivering embedded analytics.

Consider a team's engineering capability and technology integration with the rest of the data stack when developing an embedded analytics strategy. For instance, teams comfortable with advanced engineering might opt for open-source alternatives like **cube.js**. In contrast, less tech-savvy teams might prefer commercial platforms like **SiSense**.

Also critical are security considerations—including data encryption and trustworthy access controls—and the ability to customize the embedded analytics to match an organization's branding and user interface. Leading solutions will offer extensive software development kits (SDKs) to deliver such customization.

Exploring the Advantages of Augmented Analytics

When examining the future role of traditional dashboards in the Modern Data Stack, a shift becomes apparent—more and more insights are being embedded directly into operational systems in real time. This is made possible by leveraging AI and ML, which can now offer decision-makers timely and valuable insights.

These technologies have found practical applications across numerous industries and departments. For instance, AI is used to analyze buyer sentiment during sales cycles. Physicians now receive immediate feedback during medical procedures, while real-time insights about machinery maintenance have transformed industrial environments.

Each application showcases how AI and ML can enhance and augment human decision-making processes. The term "augmented analytics" refers to using these advanced models to identify patterns, generate insights, predict future trends, and suggest the best actions at critical moments within the business process.

Interaction with augmented analytics can be as straightforward as communicating with AI through a natural language interface, such as a chatbot or search tool. Examples of this can be seen with vendors like **ThoughtSpot**.

Augmented analytics can provide descriptive, diagnostic, and predictive capabilities. Descriptive analytics helps understand what happened, diagnostic analytics offers insights into why it happened, and predictive analytics forecasts what could happen.

Vendors like **Sisu**, for example, offer deep, visual explanations for changes in metrics over time. AI-powered solutions like **Anodot** can monitor critical operational processes and alert teams when anomalies, or deviations from long-term patterns, occur—enabling swift corrective action.

Signal Boost: A Telecom Titan's Leap to Analytics Democratization[7]

In a telecoms industry distinguished mainly through service quality and threatened by customer churn, one European provider found their IT team struggling to keep up with the growing internal demand for BI, analytics, and reporting.

They launched ThoughtSpot for two primary user groups: a larger one of regular dashboard users across marketing, sales, and finance, and a smaller, high-potential user group. The company set up KPIs, including time saved and user experience, to monitor the effectiveness of the rollout.

After learning from a pilot delivery, they focused on high-potential departments with an internal roadshow, demonstrating platform capabilities in various team meetings. Augmented analytics enabled users to get answers to new questions they couldn't ask before, and all the data was readily accessible for direct user search.

The company calculated about €40,000 in monthly time savings—with significant user engagement and operational efficiencies—by democratizing access to data and analytics across the company.

Data Workspaces: A Sandbox for Experts

With much attention given to data democratization and enabling the broader data literacy of an organization to grow and flourish, it's also essential to review innovations that focus on allowing the technical data specialists across a company to achieve more significant results.

In this area, data workspace tools have been making their mark on the Modern Data Stack, offering an integrated environment where data teams—including analysts, engineers, and scientists—can collaborate on data-related tasks ranging from exploration to analysis and model building. These workspaces foster seamless sharing of code, data, and insights, which enhances collaboration and productivity across traditionally siloed groups.

Such platforms streamline the entire analytics workflow, allowing multiple concurrent users to share and comment on each other's queries, reports, and dashboards. This collaborative, iterative approach improves upon traditional data analysis methods.

Figure 6.2: A Hex Data Workbench in Action[8]

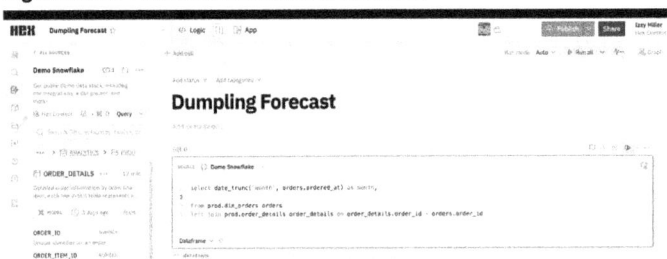

Data workspaces also integrate SQL, Python, and R, enabling users to alternate between tools as needed, making them highly versatile. The workbenches also offer modern version control features, allowing users to manage code versions and approve changes easily.

Vendors like **Hex** and **Deepnote** are currently establishing themselves in this category. However, it's uncertain if these vendors will maintain their specialized roles or if larger competitors, such as cloud service providers or major BI vendors, will absorb their functionality. For instance, ThoughtSpot acquired **Mode** in 2023.

To successfully implement a data workspace, it's necessary to understand a data team's current shortcomings, whether collaboration, workflow efficiency, or democratizing data access. Any investment in technology should be accompanied by a plan to upskill the intended users, including courses on code-based languages like SQL, R, or Python.

Lastly, a workspace could become "the Wild West" of data consumption without a proper governance strategy. Therefore, managing data access and usage within the workspace is crucial. Modern data workspace platforms offer enterprise-grade security, flexible deployment models, easy authentication, and secure database connections, all complying with regulations like SOC2 and HIPAA.

> **Boosting FinTech Flexibility through Data Workbench Integration[9]**
>
> A midsize fintech company that provides software and APIs for rapid money transfer across the global digital banking system was looking for tooling. It needed to help the company's data scientists save time on projects through better collaboration with stakeholders and to conduct more flexible analysis and ML.
>
> They chose Hex, specifically for its interoperability between SQL and Python, which allowed team members to explore SQL and build more complex models using Python while adhering to strict security and compliance rules around data access.
>
> The team explored business growth, billing, and finance using the platform. It guided product research and development and go-to-market strategies, applying data science models to determine the economic feasibility of roadmap investments. Using a flexible data workbench platform significantly improved the customer's analytical velocity, removing many of the silos between data science teams, analysts, and the business.

The Power of Analytic Application Frameworks

Beyond using commercial vendor platforms to deliver visual dashboards, embedded analytics, or augmented components, there's also a wide choice of app framework tools designed to improve productivity for teams that develop and deploy data-driven web applications.

These frameworks offer libraries and templates that allow developers and tech-savvy users to create interactive web applications for visualization, data exploration, and analysis. They often deliver more targeted or specific functionality than standard vendor dashboards or reports.

Common examples of these frameworks include **Streamlit**, which is designed specifically for building web apps against data science or ML models; **Plotly Dash**, used for constructing analytical web applications in Python; and **Shiny**, which enables the transformation of R-based analyses into interactive web applications, without requiring specialist knowledge of HTML, CSS, or JavaScript.

Figure 6.3: Streamlit Analytic Application for Financial Analysis[10]

These app frameworks allow users to build sophisticated web applications with minimal coding, enabling relatively swift assembly, testing, and publication. However, successful implementation of these frameworks calls for the ability of the operations teams to manage and maintain the apps in a production setting. This involves regularly updating underlying open-source components, handling user support, and managing change requests.

Successfully integrating these app frameworks with existing systems or tools needs to be carefully planned. Seamless integration improves the functionality of the developed applications and enhances their usability and the user experience overall.

Data Science, Machine Learning, and Artificial Intelligence

DSML & AI capabilities are growing in the heart of Modern Data Stacks, as discussed in Chapter 4. These tools enable data processing directly within data warehouses, lakes, or lakehouses (reducing the need for data movement or egress) and generate models that various analysts or user-facing tools can consume.

These tools tools help automate and simplify the process of building, deploying, and managing ML models, connecting to data sources in earlier layers of the stack, and providing features for engineering, model selection, training, evaluation, deployment, and operational monitoring. They aim to streamline the often complex workflows associated with data science, which boosts productivity and enables less technical users to interact with ML models.

Once again, these platforms are designed to help data scientists and engineers streamline the often-complex workflows involved with data science to improve productivity. They often include capabilities aimed at less-technical users (so-called "citizen data scientists") to create or interact with ML models to help broaden the use of AI within an organization.[11]

Successful DSML & AI strategies rely heavily on data quality from earlier steps in the data's journey. Data cleansing and preparation should be prioritized, as poor data quality could lead to the failure of subsequent ML models. Collaboration between data scientists, engineers, analysts, and business users is crucial for creating practical and effective models.

While building DSML & AI models takes significant effort and resources, managing and maintaining these models is an even more critical aspect of a data science strategy. Processes must be in place to manage the entire ML model lifecycle, including updating models with new data, monitoring for accuracy or potential drift, and retiring or replacing models when necessary.

It must be ensured that processes are in place for managing the entire ML model lifecycle, including how the models are updated when new data arrives, monitored for accuracy or potential drift over time, and how models are retired or replaced in due course.

To decide which DSML & AI tool is best, consider a team's needs and skill levels, the data it will be working with, and the types of problems that need to be solved.

Leading DSML & AI technologies include:

- **Databricks**: Provides a unified data analytics platform and a collaborative workspace for data scientists.
- **DataRobot**: Offers an automated ML platform that simplifies the complex steps of building DSML models.
- **Dataiku**: Provides a collaborative data science platform suitable for code-literate data scientists and business analysts.
- **AWS Sagemaker:** Offers a fully managed service that enables building, training, and deploying DSML models at scale on the Amazon cloud platform.
- **Alteryx**: Provides DSML model-building extensions to its data preparation and analysis capabilities.
- **KNIME:** Offers access to all popular AI/ML libraries through an open ecosystem.

The Emerging AI Stack: A Note of Caution

Beyond the use and consumption of data by DSML & AI tools, a rapidly evolving ecosystem of AI-specific stack capabilities is emerging. Although exciting, leaders must cautiously approach the burgeoning development in the field. Many of these novel components are riding the current wave of industry hype. Adopting them prematurely may present unforeseen challenges.

As AI progresses at an unprecedented rate, a "modern AI stack"—a comprehensive set of technologies and tools designed to support an AI pipeline—is becoming an increasingly critical part of the Modern Data Stack. This emerging AI stack includes,

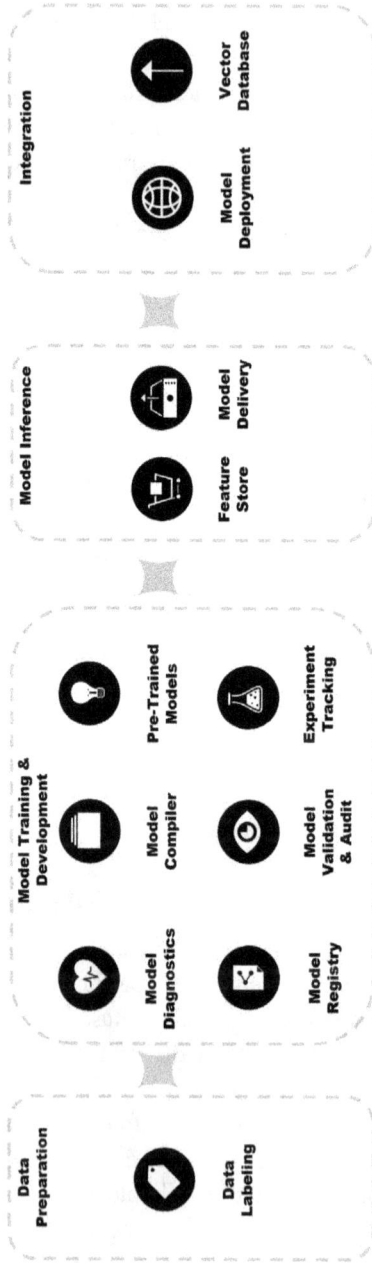

Figure 6.4: A Possible Emerging AI Stack

but is not limited to, data ingestion and preparation capabilities, model training, and validation, deployment, and monitoring capacities.

Given its growing importance and complexity, the emerging AI stack will likely receive a dedicated chapter in future editions of this TinyTechGuide. For now, even in their infancy, it's essential to build awareness of newer critical AI capabilities that have the potential to revolutionize the way data is processed and consumed.

Data Labeling

Data labeling tools have emerged due to the need for high-quality data in DSML & AI training cycles. Among other tasks, labeling activities include categorizing images, annotating text, or identifying boundaries in images.

Two primary approaches exist for data labeling. Some vendors employ trained workforces to manually label datasets, applying their domain knowledge through a collaborative management platform. This method relies heavily on human expertise but may be more time-consuming and less scalable.

In contrast, programmatic labeling employs AI to automatically label training data through user-written labeling functions. While this approach demands a more technically skilled team, it is easier to automate and scale, making it an appealing choice for larger or more complex datasets.

Current vendors providing solutions in this space include **Scale AI**, **LabelBox**, **Snorkel**, and **AWS SageMaker's Ground Truth** service.

When developing a data labeling strategy, prioritization of relevant data is essential. Not all data must be labeled, but balancing quantity and quality is crucial to prevent subpar model performance.

However, more technically challenging, programmatic data labeling can benefit significantly by automating the process and reducing manual workloads. Regular reviews and updates to labeled data are crucial to ensure ongoing relevance and accuracy.

It's also important to be mindful of potential biases in the data labeling process, as these can skew the model's performance and lead to ethical concerns. Biased data, whether due to the nature of the collected data or the labeling process itself, can result in models that unfairly favor certain outcomes or demographics, which can have significant real-world implications.

> **Picture Perfect: Transforming Image Analysis for Optimized Marketing in Luxury Brands**[12]
>
> A British luxury brand deals with a high volume of unstructured data, primarily images used in its marketing campaigns. Manual identification and labeling of these images proved unscalable, with open-source software failing to read from data sources reliably.
>
> The company selected LabelBox for tight integration with its existing data lakehouse (Databricks). Because of this integration, the company could annotate images at scale in hours instead of months. Images uploaded and tested against pre-trained DSML & AI models could predict the engagement they would receive in upcoming campaigns, leading to better decision-making.

Model Diagnostics

As DSML & AI models are trained and deployed, understanding, interpreting, and improving their performance via model diagnostics becomes increasingly vital to long-term operations.

Diagnostic tools aid in analyzing a model's performance by visualizing its behavior and identifying areas for improvement. These become crucial as models inevitably drift over time, leading to prediction inaccuracies.

When implementing model diagnostics, it's critical to identify appropriate metrics for assessing model performance. These metrics might include *accuracy* (how often the model is correct), *precision* (how often positive identifications are actually correct), *recall* (how often actual positives are identified correctly), *F1 score* (a balance of precision and recall), and *AUC-ROC* (a measurement of a classification model's quality). The choice of metrics should be discussed in depth with the data science team before deployment.

As DSML & AI models grow more opaque—for instance, large language models (LLMs) used for generative AI now contain trillions of parameters—it's increasingly important to plan for "debugging" models, as with traditional software.

This involves using model interpretation tools and diagnostics to understand why a particular prediction occurred. This helps identify potential bias or unfairness in the prediction process. This is especially critical in regulated industries, where potential bias represents a significant source of risk that data governance teams must closely monitor.

Feature Store

As organizations scale up their data science operations, moving from their first DSML & AI model into multiple production models, new challenges arise. Steps that were efficient for a single model may become less optimal when handling many models concurrently.

A feature store, a component in the emerging AI stack, helps address this issue. In ML, a "feature" refers to an input attribute that models use to make predictions. A feature store allows for the reusing and sharing of these features across different models, ensuring consistency between training, validation, and testing stages in the model lifecycle and accelerating model deployment to production.

Implementation of a feature store requires the capability to standardize features used across models. Monitoring all features is crucial to ensure their consistent performance under all scenarios. Plan for tracking feature statistics over time and be alert for abnormal changes or outlier results. Effective data management is essential, with version control for features being vital to keep track of changes and revert to earlier, stable versions if necessary.

Lastly, a good feature store should promote collaboration among data scientists across the organization. Features should be easy to discover and share within the platform, minimizing redundancy, and promoting efficient use of resources.

Pre-Trained Models

Not every data science project needs to begin from first principles. Using pre-trained models—already trained on large datasets—can provide a significant head start for many data science projects.

These models are deployed "as is" or fine-tuned to suit specific tasks, saving substantial time and computing costs. Moreover, pre-trained models can leverage the knowledge acquired from extensive and diverse datasets that may not be readily available within an organization.

Several reputable repositories of pre-trained models have emerged in recent years, primarily driven by the rise of deep learning models in the open-source community. These include:

- **HuggingFace**: Renowned for its wide array of pre-trained models for natural language processing and other applications. The Transformers library within HuggingFace contains many state-of-the-art models.
- **ModelZoo**: Houses a range of pre-trained deep learning models for tasks including image classification and object detection.
- **OpenAI**: While not necessarily as "open" as the name might suggest, OpenAI offers commercial API access to pre-trained models that can be fine-tuned, with notable strides in NLP and genAI.
- **PyTorch**: Beyond being a popular open-source deep learning framework, PyTorch hosts pre-trained models for various tasks, such as segmentation, classification, and object detection.

Using pre-trained models can significantly expedite the development and deployment of DSML & AI models. But it's essential to experiment with different pre-trained models to identify the best fit for a specific task—both in its original form and after fine-tuning.

Remember that using pre-trained models often demands considerable computer resources, including standard CPUs and often more expensive GPUs. Therefore, planning infrastructure requirements and budgets is a must.

Ethical considerations should always be at the forefront of any AI strategy. With the rise of deep learning and AI, many pre-trained models are opaque (we often simply don't know what data was used for training) and can be hard to interpret directly.[13] This opacity can be a potential roadblock for specific applications, particularly those with societal implications where biases inherent in the training data could lead to reputational risk when deployed.

Model Registry

The concept of a model registry, a centralized repository for managing DSML & AI models, has become a critical component in the emerging AI stack. It acts as a "single source of truth" for the lifecycle of models, offering scalability and control in managing ML models.

A well-structured model registry provides several benefits. It facilitates easy storage, versioning, annotation, and governance of models, which promotes consistency and ensures that everyone on the team has access to the same data and information. This centralization simplifies collaboration and accelerates the deployment of models.

Some DSML platforms have an integrated model registry, offering an all-in-one solution for managing the entire model lifecycle, such as DataRobot and Dataiku.[14] In other cases, stand-alone MLOps management platforms, such as **MLFlow** or **Neptune**, are used and often offer additional features for experimentation, reproducibility, and deployment.

Ultimately, an integrated or stand-alone model registry provides an efficient, controlled environment for managing ML models, proving invaluable for organizations that aim to scale their data science efforts.

Model Compiler

In the field of DSML & AI, it's pretty standard for models to be prototyped in Python, allowing data scientists to train and validate them against sample data. However, the actual deployment of these models often involves a different programming language or hardware environment. This is where model compilers come into play.

Model compilers act as transformers, converting initial models into highly optimized executable code that can run on specific hardware. This hardware might range from a general-purpose CPU or GPU to more specialized computer chips, such as those used in IoT devices.

Once compiled into the native language, models can operate with superior performance and lower latency when running directly on the targeted hardware. In other words, they perform much better than they would if interpreted via Python at higher levels in the computer platform.

It's important to note that the field of DSML compilers is rapidly evolving, bringing with it a certain level of uncertainty. Technologies and approaches that are top-tier today may not hold the same status tomorrow.

Therefore, when planning a model compiler strategy, it's crucial to collaborate closely with specialized hardware teams to understand the capabilities and limitations of these environments and make informed choices that maximize performance for each scenario.

Model Validation and Auditing

Model validation and auditing form the backbone of DSML & AI deployment. They help ensure the robustness and reliability of models across a broad range of scenarios. Therefore, a thorough model validation strategy is vital.

Such a strategy may incorporate components from an emerging AI stack or involve specialized validation tools, which work by testing models against various metrics like precision, recall, and F1-score (described earlier in the chapter).

Validation is crucial because it helps identify potential risks, including data drift, adversarial attacks, and other factors that could cause significant issues or perils when the model is in production.

When choosing model validation and auditing tools, prioritize those that support monitoring of model performance in both development and production environments. It is also important that these tools allow for continuous validation at regular intervals after deployment.

Model audits should offer insights into how the model makes decisions. This is not only useful for debugging but also necessary for regulatory compliance purposes. Once again, model explainability is an essential feature, allowing for regular evaluation of models for bias and fairness and ensuring they do not unjustly disadvantage any socioeconomic group.

Experiment Tracking

The process of conducting data science experiments shares many similarities with traditional scientific experiments. It requires defining a clear objective, collecting and processing relevant data, performing an experiment, iterating on the process, documenting, and publishing the findings.

These experiments often aim to gain explicit insights about a process or behavior, make forward-looking predictions based on historical data, or solve specific problems using data-driven approaches.

Data processing often involves steps discussed earlier, including data exploration, feature engineering, model selection, hyperparameter tuning, cross-validation, and performance evaluation.

As teams expand their analytical capabilities and conduct experiments at scale, DSML & AI experiment tracking tools become indispensable. These tools are designed to manage and organize the numerous experiments conducted during model development, offering capabilities such as experiment logging, parameter tracking, visualization of results, version control, and collaboration features.

These tools prevent a silo-based culture of experimentation where the findings and data from one experiment aren't shared or utilized in another. The ability to communicate and build upon the results of different experiments is a crucial feature of these tools.

Importantly, experiment tracking tools ensure the reproducibility of experiments. This allows any member of the team or an audit group to revisit and replay a DSML pipeline to achieve similar results, thereby maintaining scientific rigor and reliability.

Leading experiment tracking platforms include **Weights & Biases** and **ClearML**, which integrate with many popular data science frameworks and manage experiments through their complete lifecycle.

Growing Precision: Enhancing Agricultural Automation with Robust Machine Learning Monitoring[15]

An agricultural start-up builds robots to remove weeds from fields without damaging crops. Their approach integrates cameras, computer vision, ML, and robotics to distinguish crops from weeds in real time, using neural networks in PyTorch to analyze each frame of video and produce a pixel-accurate map locating the crops and weeds. The robot then sprays only the weeds, improving efficiency and reducing costs.

To track their ML runs, the company implemented Weights & Biases to evaluate training runs as they progressed, including interactive visualization of training and validation loss. This made communicating the latest results easy and identifying scenarios where model performance wasn't meeting expectations.

Weights & Biases also helped with reproducibility and traceability, helping teams understand the datasets used to train models, the models produced, and the model evaluation results, leading to greater control of their experimentation process.

Model Delivery

As DSML & AI models reach the deployment stage, operational aspects such as versioning, scaling, and logging become essential for successful implementation.

Application programming interface (API) endpoints are commonly used for this purpose. An API endpoint allows a model to be integrated with existing applications or services or accessed via analyst tools or code. Due to their accessibility both within and outside an organization, API endpoints are a popular implementation choice for many organizations.

Choosing the appropriate tools and frameworks to serve the model as an API endpoint involves several considerations. These include a team's expertise, existing infrastructure, the complexity of the model, and usage patterns. Cloud-based solutions are often employed, with major providers like AWS, Google Cloud, and Azure offering mechanisms for creating and serving model endpoints.

Maintaining different versions of a model via the API is crucial, as is establishing means to track a model's and API's performance. Logging plays a key role here, helping to troubleshoot and tabulate metrics such as latency, throughput, and error rates.

API endpoints, particularly those handling sensitive data, must be secured meticulously. Use authentication mechanisms and encrypted connections (for example, HyperText Transfer Protocol Secure, HTTPS), and apply rate limiting if the API is publicly accessible to prevent misuse.

Lastly, make sure that the API is well-documented. Clear and comprehensive documentation allows developers to interact effectively with the model and minimizes confusion and misuse.

Model Deployment Architectures

Models in production are complex bundles of related files, libraries, definitions, and data. They are packaged and delivered to users as a service for consumption. But beneath the surface, significant decisions need to be made regarding model maintenance, including scalability, complexity, cost, development speed, and ongoing upkeep.

Two architectures that have gained popularity with DSML & AI teams are **Docker** and serverless approaches like AWS Lambda.

Docker uses containerization technology that allows the packaging of an ML model and its dependencies into a portable container. This is a lightweight, isolated, executable package that includes everything needed to run the application consistently across different environments.

With Docker, the infrastructure and customization of the deployment environment can be controlled as needed. Docker is handy for tasks requiring environmental control, such as complex ML model deployments. However, Docker doesn't handle the orchestration process, i.e., managing how, where, and when containers run. This requires additional tools like **Docker Swarm** or **Kubernetes**.

Kubernetes (known to engineers as K8s) is an orchestration platform that manages scheduling, load balancing, and distributing containers across clusters of machines. Though robust for larger deployments, Kubernetes can be complex and unnecessary for small projects and teams.

In contrast, serverless is a model where a cloud service provider manages the infrastructure and automatically provisions and scales resources based on demand. In the DSML context, serverless platforms execute ML model predictions as simple functions.

This lets developers focus on the ML model logic without worrying about server or resource management. Serverless is particularly suitable for tasks that do not run continuously, since only the time code executes is billable.

However, serverless functions may experience delayed response after a period of inactivity (known as a "cold start"), which can impact performance. Moreover, serverless platforms often limit execution time, which may not be suitable for long-running ML tasks. Furthermore, serverless platforms are typically linked to specific cloud providers, potentially leading to vendor lock-in.

When planning model deployment architecture, consider the project's size and performance requirements. Due to better control over resources and scaling, Docker/Kubernetes may be more suitable for larger, high-performance requirements. However, serverless might be more cost-effective for smaller or infrequent services, as the cloud provider manages the infrastructure.

Combining these technologies could also be the best solution. For instance, using Docker containers orchestrated by Kubernetes for some services and serverless functions for others.

Vector Databases

Vector data is prevalent in various ML tasks, including classification, regression, clustering, and recommendation systems. Each vector in a dataset represents an individual data point (for instance, a customer) and the values within the vector correspond to specific features or attributes of that data point, such as household income, credit score, etc.

Also known as vector search engines, vector databases are specialized and designed to handle vector data efficiently. They are used extensively in scenarios that require similarity searches, such as finding kindred images, documents, users, or product recommendations on an e-commerce platform.

They use techniques like approximate nearest neighbor (ANN), which swiftly identifies data points most similar to a given query. This is particularly useful when handling large or complex datasets, as seen in modern genAI solutions.

Prominent vendors include **Pinecone** (a managed service for vector search that integrates with standard data science tools through straightforward APIs) and **Milvus** (an open-source vector database). There's also **Faiss**, a vector search library developed by Facebook AI that provides the core functionality for similarity search rather than a fully managed database service.

Remember that a vector database is a specialized tool within the emerging AI stack. Vector databases efficiently handle specific data types (vectors) and vector-based operations. Still, they should not be considered a replacement for analytical data ware-houses or transactional databases.

Practical Advice and Next Steps

- Adopt an audience-centric approach to consumption, with clear, simple visuals that help users make better decisions. Remember that these dashboards or reports aren't "one-and-done" but iterative deliverables that improve over time.
- Consider shifting from isolated dashboards and static reports towards embedding real-time insights directly into operational systems. This approach brings clean, enriched data closer to where day-to-day decisions get made.
- As new tools and technologies are adopted, train every team member on their usage and benefits. Data literacy is critical to deriving maximum value from an investment in the Modern Data Stack.
- As analytic maturity improves, explore DSML & AI capabilities that can automate or streamline existing business processes or use data in new, competitive ways.
- Prioritize data quality as a critical prerequisite for DSML & AI, ensuring that data cleansing and preparation processes are transparent and efficient.
- The full DSML & AI lifecycle is complex and evolving fast. Be aware of the many stack components needed to train, publish, update, monitor, and retire DSML & AI models in a production environment. Make small, incremental bets while AI is at the peak of inflated expectations.[16]

Summary

As this chapter illustrated, the breadth of tools and methods available for data analysis, output, and consumption is pivotal in leveraging the full potential of the Modern Data Stack. These tools transform raw data into valuable insights that drive business decisions.

It's no longer enough to store and process data alone. How it is visualized, explored, shared, and interacts with models of businesses, customers, and ecosystems can fundamentally alter the course of decision-making processes.

In business intelligence and dashboarding, tools have evolved and adapted to meet new business demands. These solutions are becoming increasingly intuitive and user-friendly, helping users to better understand and interact with data. The emergence of embedded analytics has enabled the seamless integration of visual insights directly into operational applications, reducing friction for business users.

The latest advances in AI, particularly NLP, have allowed augmented analytics platforms to reach wider audiences without deep technical expertise. At the same time, the cloud continues to offer collaborative environments for analysts to share data pipelines, automated analytic workflows, and reusable modules.

Most significantly, the evolution of the modern AI stack—built upon the foundations of data science, ML, and AI platforms—has been stark. These platforms not only enable the building of robust ML models but also the management and auditing of critical business assets throughout their lifecycle.

In the penultimate chapter, the components required to support, stabilize, and supercharge the capabilities that have been discussed will be explored, including elements like data catalogs, entitlements, access controls, and observability—including their roles in optimizing the flow of data into insights and value.

These operational functions form the bedrock of the Modern Data Stack, providing consistency, reliability, security, transparency, and trust in the data throughout its journey.

Chapter 6 References

[1] Foote, Keith D. "A Brief History of Business Intelligence." DATAVERSITY. June 6, 2023. https://www.dataversity.net/brief-history-business-intelligence/.

[2] "What Is Business Intelligence?" IBM. Accessed August 28, 2023. https://www.ibm.com/topics/business-intelligence.

[3] "The Well Reduced Turnaround Time of Data Delivery to

Clients by 90% with Sigma." Sigma. Accessed August 13, 2023. https://www.sigmacomputing.com/customer-stories/the-well-reduced-turnaround-time-of-data-delivery-to-clients-by-90-with-sigma.

4 "Dashboards Are Dead." ThoughtSpot. Accessed August 13, 2023. https://go.thoughtspot.com/e-book-dashboards-are-dead.html.

5 "Death of the Dashboard: What It Really Means for Analytics." Yellowfin. March 11, 2021. https://www.yellowfinbi.com/blog/what-death-of-dashboard-really-means-for-analytics.

6 Howson, Cindi, and Rita Sallam. "Survey Analysis: Why BI and Analytics Adoption Remains Low and How to Expand Its Reach." Gartner. June 30, 2017. https://www.gartner.com/en/documents/3753469.

7 "Self-Service with ThoughtSpot Helps T-Mobile Netherlands Sustain Market Leadership by Boosting Analyst Productivity and Cutting IT Costs." ThoughtSpot. Accessed August 28, 2023. https://media.thoughtspot.com/pdf/ThoughtSpot-T-Mobile-Case-Study.pdf.

8 "Do More with Data, Together." Hex. Accessed August 13, 2023. https://hex.tech/.

9 "Modern Treasury." Hex. Accessed August 13, 2023. https://hex.tech/customers/modern-treasury/.

0 https://gerardrbentley-fidelity-account-overview-app-ezld5n.streamlit.app/ [This page does not appear to be functional.] Image courtesy of "App Gallery." Snowflake. https://streamlit.io/gallery.

11 Stedman, Craig, and Laura Fitzgibbons. "What Is a Citizen Data Scientist and Why Are They Important?" Business Analytics. Accessed August 13, 2023. https://www.techtarget.com/ searchbusinessanalytics/definition/citizen-data-scientist.

12 "Burberry." Databricks. January 19, 2023. https://www.databricks.com/customers/burberry.

13 Bommasani, Rishi, Kevin Klyman, Daniel Zhang, and Percy

Liang. "Stanford CRFM." Stanford University. June 15, 2023. https://crfm.stanford.edu/2023/06/15/eu-ai-act.html.

[14] "Workspace Model Registry on Databricks." Databricks. June 26, 2023. https://docs.databricks.com/mlflow/model-registry.html.

[15] PyTorch. "AI for AG: Production Machine Learning for Agriculture." Medium. August 6, 2020. https://medium.com/pytorch/ai-for-ag-production-machine-learning-for-agriculture-e8cfdb9849a1.

[16] "Interpreting Technology Hype." Gartner. Accessed August 13, 2023. https://www.gartner.co.uk/ en/methodologies/gartner-hype-cycle#.

Chapter 7

Supporting Functions

In previous chapters, the focus has been on capabilities closely related to distinct phases of the Modern Data Stack. In this chapter, however, the focus is on functionality that spans the entire data lifecycle.

These capabilities may not capture immediate attention (like some more overhyped technologies in the stack) yet they form a critical backbone that supports improved data usage, governance processes, and robust and secure data pipelines. They are integral to any modern data strategy and should not be overlooked.

Our discussion begins with the evolution of data catalogs. Once static repositories, these catalogs have transformed, serving as platforms to discover, document, and curate valuable business data across individuals, teams, and divisions. They leverage metadata—the information describing the data—in innovative and active ways.

Data curation forms a part of a larger data governance strategy that builds value for future projects. Therefore, it is an element of strategic importance that should be examined.

Next, contemporary tools for managing entitlements and security—which are critical in preventing data leakage and potential damage as data moves through pipelines—are explored.

Lastly, the emerging topic of data observability is covered. With the exponential growth in data volumes and increasing complexity of data architectures, managing data health proactively has become necessary. Teams strive to identify problems as they happen or before they occur, making this topic essential to managing the Modern Data Stack.

Figure 7.1: **High-Level Functions that Support the Modern Data Stack**

Data Discovery: Unveiling Insights from the Depths of Data

Businesses often struggle to navigate, search, and understand the data within their systems, despite the extensive capabilities of the architecture discussed so far. Data discovery platforms integrate closely with existing technologies, aiming to solve this problem. They typically include:

- **Data Cataloging**: An approach to organizing a shared inventory of data assets in the organization, with metadata stored in a way that describes the sources, formats, content, and context throughout its lifecycle.
- **Data Discovery**: The ability to search and explore data assets to comprehend structure, relationships, and meaning across various business subject areas. Modern platforms use

ML to enrich and share insights based on specific data patterns.

- **Data Governance**: A broad set of capabilities managing how data is made available for wider secure use in enterprise systems, including data stewardship, privacy, and security.

Data Catalogs

Data catalogs, while serving as a curated inventory of data assets, have evolved significantly since their inception. Originally, they were manual, paper-based systems, much like library card catalogs (if you know what those are). They used rudimentary forms of metadata, akin to the Dewey Decimal System, to help users locate data.

With the advent of the digital era, data catalogs focused on metadata about database tables, fields, and relationships, corresponding closely to the emerging relational database management systems they curated. The development of data warehouses led to more sophisticated catalogs encompassing technical and business metadata.

The variety of data sources expanded substantially in the early 2000s, leading to attempts to create enterprise-wide metadata repositories. These attempts were often met with significant challenges due to large organizations' complexity and diversity of data.

As a response, modern data catalogs have become more automated, leveraging ML algorithms to classify and organize data. They provide comprehensive data information, including sources, transformation history, associated business terms, data quality metrics, and user reviews. Discovery is facilitated through search and recommendation functionalities.

Modern catalogs and discovery platforms have moved far beyond their roots, incorporating user-experience features that mirror social media platforms. Users can now "follow" datasets, receive updates, ask questions, and collaborate directly within the platform.

Enhancing Utility Services with Modern Data Discovery and Governance[1]

An electric and gas utility provider operating in the Pacific Northwest implemented data discovery as part of a Modern Data Stack to improve the company's services and products.

Data governance was a significant focus to ensure data was collected on time and at the level of completeness and detail required to answer questions. They deployed **Alation** to crawl data sources and return metadata about what was discovered, providing analysts with a comprehensive understanding of the data used.

To encourage people to adopt these new practices, a significant amount of time was spent educating people on data, listening to their perspectives, and sharing what the data revealed.

Alation also enables the open exchange of information, allowing analysts to share SQL code, write articles about their expert knowledge, and make all this information fully searchable and easily accessible.

An effective data discovery strategy requires clearly defined goals, not merely deploying a vendor solution. Whether the objective is to improve data governance, enhance data quality, assist with data integration, or support data-driven decision-making, having a clear vision is crucial.

Long-term planning for a data catalog requires an understanding that data requirements will likely grow and evolve. Scalability—particularly the ability to handle increasing volumes and a variety of data—should be a factor in the early stages of a project. Before committing to a platform solution, consider piloting it with smaller user groups to evaluate the functionality and to gather direct feedback.

With analytic automation a priority for many data leaders, ML should be leveraged to automate as many aspects of data cataloging as possible. For instance, it is a wise choice to find vendors that can automatically classify data, suggest relevant datasets, and detect sensitive data without continual human intervention. This will reduce the manual effort required to maintain the data catalog, ensuring that the catalog stays up-to-date as data changes and evolves.

Data Governance: For a Strong Foundation

Data governance encompasses the processes, policies, standards, and technologies that manage data assets across organizations. Its main goal is to ensure data quality through all components in a Modern Data Stack and to guarantee data and its controls align with company policies and regulatory requirements, such as GDPR or HIPAA.

Within governance teams, data stewards play a crucial role. They are responsible for data quality and implementation of governance policies at the operational level and act as liaisons between technology, data, and business units.

A Data Marketplace Fuels Accelerating Insights for a Global Automotive Giant[2]

For one of the world's largest providers of automotive services and solutions, there were challenges around taming the data from such a large, geographically dispersed brand. To address these, the company created a data marketplace using **Collibra** that served as a one-stop shop for data.

This marketplace enabled users to discover data they didn't even know existed within the company. The adoption of Collibra accelerated rapidly, with new datasets added every week. The marketplace exposed over 300,000 columns from over 5,000 tables across 300-plus datasets to over 1,500 individual users who queried the database over 5 million times monthly.

The company plans to grow from this foundation and enhance data quality, automate more processes, and expand its marketplace with more governed data sources to drive value across the business.

Master data management (MDM) often falls under the responsibility of data governance teams. MDM software supports the creation and management of a single, consistent definition of crucial data entities in an organizational context, such as customer, product, or supplier.

Investing in a data governance strategy significantly enhances an organization's capabilities to manage data effectively. Consequently, a governance platform becomes essential to the Modern Data Stack. It's necessary to carefully define and agree upon roles, responsibilities, data standards, and policies across stakeholders.

Many organizations establish a *data governance council*, including representatives from all areas of the organization with a stake in managing data.[3] This typically encompasses leaders from various business units, IT, and other departments that heavily use data. The idea is to consider all perspectives when making governance decisions.

One of the critical roles of this senior group is to advocate for data governance across the organization. This can involve communicating the value of such governance to employees, training on policies and procedures, and fostering a culture of data stewardship and literacy.

Entitlements and Security: Safeguards and Protections

Data entitlements and security are closely interlinked. Good data entitlement practices significantly enhance data security, while failure to manage data entitlements effectively can lead to severe breaches and compliance issues.

Entitlements specify who can access specific data within the organization and the actions they are permitted to carry out with it. These actions can include viewing, editing, deleting, or sharing, with permissions often defined based on existing organizational roles. The level of access is determined at various levels of granularity, from access to an entire database down to individual rows of data.

Security involves integrity, availability, ensuring confidentiality, and safeguarding data from unauthorized access and breaches. Data security can encompass techniques like encryption (for data that is in motion or at rest), anonymization, access controls, and auditing.

Implementing an entitlements and security strategy involves working closely with architects and data governance and security teams across the Modern Data Stack. Strive to enforce role-based access controls to manage data based on business needs. Aim to follow the "principle of least privilege" — limiting access rights for users to the bare minimum permissions they need to perform their work duties—and expand cautiously from there.

Continuous monitoring of data access and usage is essential to the detection of emerging security threats. Moreover, a plan to respond to data breaches or security incidents—encompassing initial identification, containment, investigation, and prevention of similar future events—is a necessity.

Most importantly, invest in regular training and upskilling of employees on security, best practices, and the importance of data protection. Make sure they know the risks associated with data breaches and their crucial role in preventing them.

Data Observability: The Health of the Data Stack in Focus

In the context of the Modern Data Stack, observability serves as a metric for the performance, health, and reliability of software components and data pipelines. It facilitates faster detection and resolution of issues.

Generally, observability falls into three categories:

- **Logs**: Records of discrete events over time.
- **Metrics:** Numerical data measured over intervals of time that provide a simple way to view the system's behavior. For example, the number of transactions processed in the last hour.
- **Traces:** Used to understand the complete lifecycle of a transaction or business operation rather than discrete events.

An effective data observability strategy should incorporate proactive system monitoring to identify potential issues before they escalate into major problems. It should include alerting and remediation steps to aid in resolving outages or failures.

Modern observability platforms like **Monte Carlo** and **Bigeye** leverage ML to proactively identify data issues, assess their impact, and automatically notify relevant stakeholders. They often include sophisticated anomaly detection and lineage-driven root cause and impact analysis, which involves tracing issues back to their origin to understand and address their impact.

The open-source tool **Great Expectations** has fostered a growing community around data quality testing within data pipelines. Great Expectations is a Python-based library that allows teams to define assertions about the properties of data. For example, a certain column should always be unique, or a date field should always be in the past. These expectations form a contract for expected data quality. The tool can validate observed data against this contract.

Practical Advice and Next Steps

- Don't make data discovery an afterthought when planning!
- Prioritize and develop a data cataloging strategy early in the design of the data architecture, preferably when still working with only a few data sources.
- Make sure to plan for automation so the catalog is always up-to-date, and prioritize augmented features such as au-

tomatic classification, dataset recommendations, and au-
to-detection of sensitive data sources.

- Aim to pilot a data catalog platform with a small, active
segment of the user base early in the rollout of a stack.
- Educate stakeholders on the value of data governance early
on, explaining the value of defined roles, responsibilities,
data standards, and general policies. Use this to grow a culture of data stewardship, leading to a data governance council with representatives from across the organization.
- Implement role-based access controls and follow the "principle of least privilege."
- Regularly monitor data access and usage, providing regular
training on data security best practices. In the meantime,
have a data breach response plan defined and ready.
- Make data observability a priority. Implement system monitoring, alerting, and remediation steps to help resolve incidents, outages, or failures.

Summary

This chapter explored the often-unsung heroes of the Modern
Data Stack: data discovery, cataloging, governance, observability,
and robust security measures. While these components may not
always be at the forefront of user attention or business budgets,
they are pivotal in cultivating a culture of trust, security, and value around an organization's digital assets.

As data architectures become increasingly complex, proactive
data health management becomes essential. Modern data science,
ML, and AI techniques can significantly augment a data team's
ability to anticipate issues, assess their impact, and maintain service levels for a diverse range of consumers and business stakeholders.

The final chapter will address the challenges and criticisms
of implementing Modern Data Stack tools and frameworks. By
sharing perspectives from vocal community members, the aim is
to provide a balanced view of the current landscape.

Additionally, the potential trends and newer frameworks that could reshape increasingly data-driven business environments will be explored. Which of these will genuinely shape the future of the Modern Data Stack?

Chapter 7 References

[1] "How Alation Helped Avista Understand Their Data: A Fundamental Requirement." Alation. June 16, 2023. https://www.alation.com/resource-center/customer-case-studies/how-alation-helped-avista-understand-their-data-a-fundamental-requirement/.

[2] Collibra. "Cox Automotive Leverages Collibra to Provide Employees with a One-Stop Shop for All Things Data." YouTube Video. October 31, 2022. https://www.youtube.com/watch? v=nYxRIXSqIXM.

[3] "Data Governance Council: What Is It and Why Do You Need One?" Collibra. September 16, 2021. https://www.collibra.com/us/en/blog/data-governance-council-what-is-it-and-why-do-you-need-one.

Chapter 8

The Future of the Modern Data Stack

The Modern Data Stack is a testament to the extraordinary progress made in data management and analytics technology. This leap forward results from concerted innovation in hardware, software, user-experience design, and the widespread adoption of cloud computing.

Flexible and scalable by design, the Modern Data Stack caters to the increasingly intricate needs of today's data and analytics teams—it is a highly modular architecture composed of various technologies, each specialized to handle tasks within the larger data ecosystem, from data ingestion and storage to processing and visualization.

Like building blocks, these components can be assembled and reassembled to create a data infrastructure that fits an organization's unique needs and objectives. This flexibility—married with the scalability to manage growing data volumes, varieties, and velocities—ensures that data architecture remains agile and capable of evolving with organizational growth.

Stress Points of the Modern Data Stack

While the Modern Data Stack offers substantial flexibility and scalability, it isn't without critics or challenges. Indeed, this approach is not universally considered the cure-all for data analytics teams.

Critics suggest that its highly compartmentalized nature could lead to added complexity and increased operational overhead. Each tool or service in the stack must be configured, integrated, and managed—a process requiring significant time and resources.

Additionally, the costs of these services can spike with increased data volumes, rendering the return on investment (ROI) challenging to determine. Businesses may be locked into certain vendors since migration to different services could require significant time and effort.

Despite advancements in data management and analytics technology, this approach still does not eliminate the age-old challenges surrounding data quality, security, and privacy. The stack's efficacy depends on the quality of the data it handles. Furthermore, securing sensitive data and maintaining privacy within complex data architectures remains daunting.

A Modern Data Stack implementation also demands a roster of skilled professionals on project teams who can navigate the intricacies of this evolving landscape. These skill sets are often in high demand, leading to talent shortages in the market.

Cost Concerns: Data Movement without Breaking the Bank

While cloud-based data solutions may initially seem cost-effective, they can quickly turn expensive as data volumes increase. This is particularly true for solutions that charge customers based on data volume or query-computation time.

Calculating charges based on compute time, complex queries, or inefficient use of resources can lead to unexpectedly high bills. Hence, it's crucial to fully understand the pricing model of any solution and monitor usage to avoid cost overruns.

One critical but often overlooked aspect is the cost of moving data between different parts of the stack. These costs can add up quickly, especially if not considered in the initial budgeting. They are typically linked to data egress, which refers to the outflow of data from a network, and are usually billed per gigabyte.

Data transfer within the same virtual network (VNET)—an isolated section in the cloud—is generally free if the services are closely located. However, data flowing into or out of other cloud regions incurs charges, ranging from $0.05 to $0.20 per GB (at the time of writing), depending on the cloud provider and the region.

While these costs may seem trivial at the gigabyte scale, they can rapidly escalate when dealing with the regular movement of terabytes or petabytes per project, amounting to hundreds of thousands of dollars in data movement costs alone.

It's essential to understand both the functional architecture (the components and building blocks) and the physical architecture (the cloud regions and services used to deliver the data stack) and optimize data flow to manage these costs.

This could include deploying resources in regions with lower data transfer costs, limiting cross-zone and cross-region data transfers, optimizing the architecture of applications to minimize data travel paths, and compressing or deduplicating data before movement.

Cost Concerns: Pay-per-Row and Compute Credits

Many vendors choose monthly pricing models based on the number of rows of data processed, transferred, or stored. While this may be advantageous for smaller businesses or those with predictable data usage, it can be difficult for larger organizations to forecast costs due to fluctuations and potential spikes in data usage, leading to surprisingly high costs.

Critics, like Lauren Balik, argue that these vendors often exhibit "rent-seeking behavior," a business model that charges customers more without providing equivalent value.[1] For instance, vendors charging based on the number of active rows ingested results in customers being billed multiple times for a single activity.

Similarly, connectors creating over 60 tables of extracted source data from complex applications can lead to disproportionate costs relative to actual activity. Balik claims that vendors may encourage data practices and processes that are deliberately computationally expensive, potentially inflating these vendors' popularity and valuation in the startup market.

Another cost concern arises from purchasing large compute credits from cloud service providers. Initial discounts or bundled offerings can entice companies to commit to more cloud resources than they need.

These credits often have a use-it-or-lose-it policy, where unused credits are forfeited after a certain period, usually a year, leading to wastage as companies end up paying for resources they don't utilize.

Interestingly, cloud computing costs for the Modern Data Stack are somewhat paradoxical. Initially, cloud services offered cheaper execution and greater scalability, driving operational efficiencies and fostering innovation because resources could be focused on growth and product development.

However, as a company's use of cloud services matures, the scale of data storage, processing, and consumption can pressure margins and start to outweigh the benefits, especially when growth starts to slow. Unfortunately, reversing this shift can be challenging because of the years of technical investment made in new features—but not infrastructure optimization.

In extreme cases, some companies resort to "repatriating" workloads, moving them from the cloud back to on-premises data centers, or adopting a hybrid approach to realize operational cost savings.[2]

Calculating Return on Investment for the Modern Data Stack

Many data teams find themselves grappling with the sunk costs of existing DIY-style projects, often built by a few talented data engineers using open-source platforms. Transitioning from these homemade tools to a professional, end-to-end data analytics solution allows analysts and engineers to focus on their primary responsibilities: extracting and using data insights to drive business improvement.

Yet, how is the actual return on this significant investment measured?

Fundamentally, the components should align with business objectives. If cost reduction is the goal, the emphasis should be on streamlining processes and automating tasks.

If revenue growth is the focus, investment should lean towards embedded and augmented analytics that directly contribute to the company's go-to-market strategy or efforts to reduce customer churn.

Approaches like the "Data Science Value Engineering Framework" proposed by Bill Schmarzo and Kirk Borne in *The Economics of Data, Analytics, and Digital Transformation* offer practical guidance.[3] This framework helps businesses harness their data analytics technologies to enhance operations and foster collaboration between business domain experts and data teams.

Even experts such as PWC claim that measuring ROI in data and AI projects can be tricky.[4] They suggest that returns can be viewed as "hard" (such as cost savings, time savings, productivity increases, and revenue growth) or "soft" (such as enhanced customer experience, improved skills retention, and increased organizational agility).

Common pitfalls to avoid when calculating ROI for data-related initiatives include oversimplifying the benefits of predictive models by ignoring the impact of these models making mistakes, measuring ROI at a single point in time rather than over a longer window, and assessing projects in isolation instead of as part of a portfolio investment across multiple functions.

Looking to the Future: Trends and Emerging Practices

Data Mesh

Emerging as an alternative to the Modern Data Stack, the data mesh architecture emphasizes decentralization, domain-oriented data ownership and governance, and viewing data as a product in its own right rather than simply a by-product of other software processes.[5]

The data mesh model rethinks the traditional concept of data flowing through pipelines to a centralized repository, as in the case of a data warehouse or lake. Instead, data is distributed across various domains. Each domain is under the ownership and management of a cross-functional team composed of members from different areas of expertise, all of whom have an intimate understanding of the data and its context.

These specialized data teams are entrusted with the quality and usability of the data within their area of knowledge. This approach effectively decomposes a complicated, inefficient data ecosystem into smaller, independent services. This is similar to the microservice architecture used in software development, and it reflects the broader tech industry's focus on decentralization, autonomy, and domain-driven design.

Data contracts, which define the interface for data access and use, allow data consumers to understand what they're receiving, how they can use it, and what they can expect from each "data product."

The transition to a data mesh architecture is challenging. It likely requires significant changes in organizational culture, such as decentralization, that can disturb existing political and organizational structures.

This model requires more trust in distributed teams' ability to effectively manage their data and comply with organizational data governance policies. Moreover, it strongly emphasizes standardization and coordination among different teams, all significant attributes in mature analytic cultures.

DataOps/MLOps

DataOps, a discipline that marries the principles of Agile, DevOps, and Lean management practices, has seen rapid growth in recent years. It aims to enhance the speed and quality of data analytics operations. Its influence in the industry continues to expand.

Providing significant benefits to organizations—such as improved data quality, shorter development cycles, and more efficient workflows—DataOps encourages continuous testing, monitoring, and deployment of data pipelines, which fosters an agile and responsive data environment.

Implementing DataOps may present specific challenges, such as organizational resistance to change and the need for specialized skills. Companies may also need to invest in new tools and technologies to support a DataOps approach.

Similarly, MLOps applies these best practices to the ML lifecycle. MLOps aims to adopt a mindset of continuous improvement, a core tenet of DevOps practice, focusing on building, supporting, and maintaining DSML & AI pipelines as long-term competitive advantages for organizations. This practice recognizes that ML models are not one-time projects but ongoing processes that require regular updates, maintenance, and monitoring.

Data as Code

Embracing principles from the world of DevOps and modern software engineering, the "data as code" philosophy is gaining traction within the realm of the Modern Data Stack.[6]

With this approach, various aspects of data management—including data structures, schemas, and configurations—are treated much like code. They can be version-controlled, tested, and automated, freeing them from being tied to specific vendors' implementations. This offers several key advantages, including improved collaboration, increased efficiency, and reduced errors.

Tools that support the "data as code" paradigm, such as dbt and Apache Airflow, have become commonplace. They enable teams to build workflows and author, schedule, and monitor data transformations programmatically. This, in turn, enhances the reliability of these processes and reduces the costs associated with changes.

For instance, version control allows teams to track and manage changes to data structures and configurations, ensuring that any modifications can be easily traced and, if necessary, reversed. Automated testing ensures that changes do not introduce errors, thereby increasing the overall quality of the data.

However, as with DevOps and MLOps, adopting the "data as code" approach also presents challenges. It requires a culture shift within the organization. Adopting new tools and workflows can initially increase complexity. Nonetheless, the potential benefits of this paradigm make it a promising trend for the future of data management.

Zero ETL

In the traditional ETL process, data is extracted from various sources, ingested, and loaded into data processing platforms before being transformed and prepared for analysis. This transformation step can be complex, time-consuming, and require substantial cloud-computing resources, especially with large data volumes.

Zero ETL introduces a streamlined alternative that aims to minimize transformation. Instead, data is extracted and loaded into the data storage layer in its raw state without intermediate steps for transformation or cleaning.

This approach yields several benefits. First, it significantly speeds up the data ingestion as the transformation step is eliminated. Second, the simplicity of Zero ETL can reduce overall data management complexity, leading to potential cost savings.

It may also preserve data quality and integrity by reducing data manipulation.

However, Zero ETL also comes with limitations, such as restricted data transformation capabilities when dealing with more complex data structures or mappings. It may need help to integrate with systems outside the existing ecosystem.

Major cloud platform vendors are beginning to adopt Zero ETL. For instance, **AWS Aurora** and AWS Redshift, as well as **Google Bigtable**, allow transactional data to be immediately available in a data warehouse in its raw form.

Incorta offers near real-time reporting and analytics directly from original transactional data outside these major players, circumventing the need for complex data modeling or ETL processing.

Zero ETL represents a trend toward more efficient, raw data-focused processes in the Modern Data Stack context. However, it still requires careful implementation to ensure data remains accessible and usable for various business needs.

The Impact of the AI Revolution on Data Infrastructure

The increasing use of AI, particularly LLMs like ChatGPT, **Bard**, **Claude**, and others, is transforming the landscape of data infrastructure, including the Modern Data Stack. These AI models require vast processing power and storage, which presents significant challenges to data management infrastructure and can substantially increase operating costs.

As these AI models evolve, they are growing in complexity and size, often exceeding a trillion parameters. While vital for their function, this size of model can strain operational budgets with the need for advanced, costly hardware and compute resources.

Despite the ongoing innovation in AI algorithm design and efficiency, the sheer scale and cost of such generative AI models will likely disrupt the near future. Solutions to mitigate these challenges are emerging, such as developing highly optimized or even simpler, specialized models that can reduce both the model sizes in the cloud and the workload in data centers.

One such approach is distributing generative AI applications workload to consumer devices like smartphones and PCs, reducing the burden on corporate budgets. An example of this comes from HuggingFace, which demonstrated smaller ChatGPT-like LLMs (the 30 billion parameter Vicuna-30B and the 13 billion parameter Vicuna-13B) capable of running on a single consumer device.[7]

This transition to more decentralized processing can help manage data center costs and open up new possibilities for using AI in everyday devices. However, addressing potential drawbacks—such as the security and privacy concerns raised by distributing the workload to consumer devices—is crucial. Navigating the future of AI and data infrastructure will likely involve a balanced blend of centralized and decentralized solutions.

Can a Single Vendor Make the Modern Data Stack More Manageable?

It's understandable if you're feeling slightly overwhelmed after diving into the complexities of the Modern Data Stack.

The current landscape is densely packed with a vast array of data and analytics services. While each component can simplify and reduce the cost of its specific function, customers often find themselves responsible for integrating these disparate parts into a coherent whole. This process can become a significant source of expense, as it often necessitates engaging professional services.

Cloud service providers like AWS, Google, and Azure recognize this issue and have begun bundling combinations of services that are frequently used in conjunction. These bundles offer seamless integrations, promotional pricing, and professional services tied into a single offering. This approach incentivizes customers to engage with a specific provider's platform, as it offers a more streamlined and cost-effective solution.

Below are several contemporary solution architectures that cover the complete Modern Data Stack functionality from the perspective of a single vendor.

Table 8.1: Comparing Functional Capabilities of Major Cloud Service Providers

Function	AWS	Azure	Google Cloud
Ingestion & Transport	AWS IoT, Kinesis, Glue	Azure Data Factory, Event Hub	Cloud IoT, PubSub
Storage, Query, & Processing	Glacier, S3, RDS, Redshift, DynamoDB, ElasticSearch	Azure Synapse, Azure Data Lake Store, Cosmos DB	BigQuery, BigTable
Transformation	Glue	Azure Data Factory	DataProc, DataPrep, DataFlow
Analytics Output	Sagemaker, QuickSight	Power BI, Azure ML	DataLab, AutoML, DataStudio
Supporting Functions	Glue Catalog	Data Catalog	Data Catalog

A few functional architecture diagrams for the major providers outlined above will now be shared.

AWS Solution Architecture

Figure 8.1: Sample Modern Data Stack Solution Architecture with Amazon

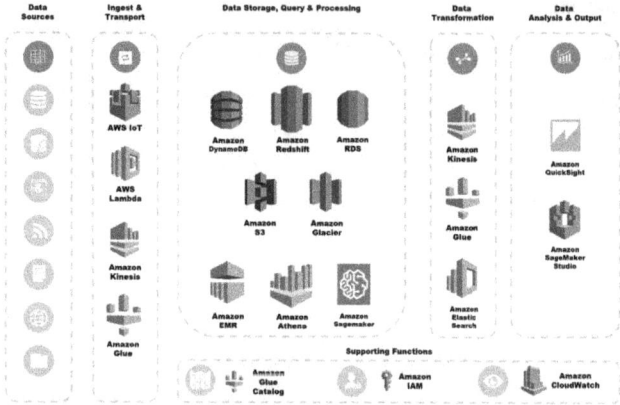

Azure Solution Architecture

Figure 8.2: Sample Modern Data Stack Solution Architecture with Azure

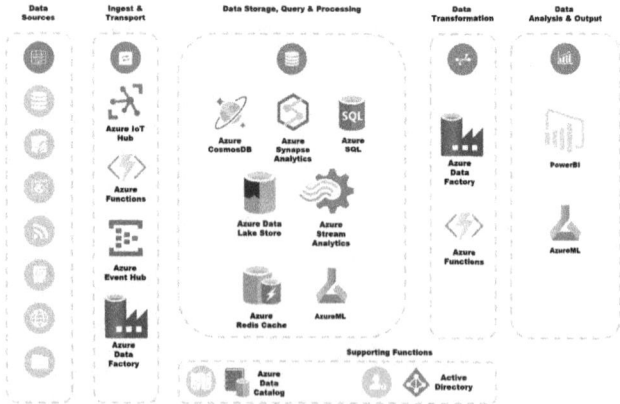

Google Cloud Solution Architecture

Figure 8.3: Sample Modern Data Stack Solution Architecture with Google Cloud

Microsoft Fabric Solution Architecture

Microsoft made waves in 2023 by introducing its unified analytics platform, **Microsoft Fabric**.[8] This end-to-end platform claims to simplify the data analytics stack by integrating existing technologies like **Azure Data Factory**,[9] Azure Synapse Analytics,[10] and Power BI into a single ecosystem.

Fabric also includes a built-in multi-cloud data lake called **OneLake**,[11] which is automatically available to every Fabric tenant. OneLake supports structured data of any format, as well as unstructured data, which further simplifies the data management process.

In a move that leverages the power of AI, Fabric integrates the **Azure OpenAI Service**[12] throughout its stack in a move that leverages AI's power. This delivers an AI-powered "copilot" to assist engineers and analysts in creating data pipelines, generating code, and building ML models using natural language.

Fig 8.5: Sample Modern Data Stack Solution Architecture with Microsoft Fabric

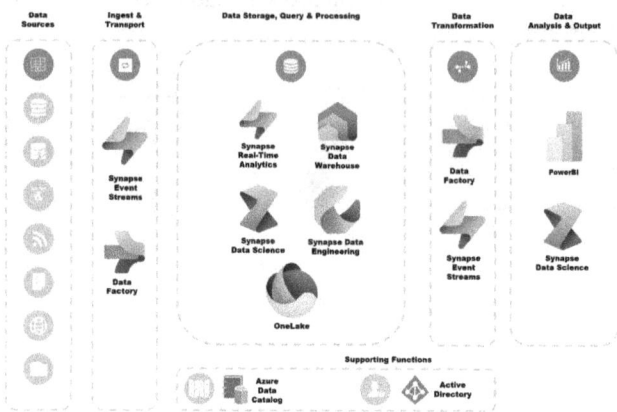

This trend towards simplifying and bundling services presents an exciting evolution in the landscape. It indicates a future where navigating the complexities of data and analytics could become a much more streamlined, intuitive, and cost-effective process.

Practical Advice and Next Steps

- Pay extremely close attention to costs, especially data transfer, storage, and compute time. Look to optimize data pipelines and limit data transfers across cloud zones to keep costs under control. If practical, Consider deploying resources in cloud regions with lower data transfer costs.
- Measure ROI in "hard" terms (cost/time savings and commercial opportunities) versus "soft" terms like improved customer experience and organizational agility.
- Avoid pitfalls like oversimplifying the benefits of predictive models or measuring ROI at a single point in time. Consider frameworks like Schmarzo and Borne's "Data Science Value Engineering Framework" for guidance.
- Assess the readiness and business appetite for decentralization, e.g., shift to a data mesh architecture for one or more pilot projects, then proceed cautiously and incrementally.
- Identify areas of data analytics operations that could bene-

fit from more automation and quicker development cycles and implement DataOps principles in those areas.

- Consider the bundled services offered by major cloud providers offering unified data stacks and services that can streamline data operations and potentially reduce costs.
- Given the increasing value of AI use cases, and the challenges that AI presents to data infrastructure, staying ahead of the curve is crucial. Adopt a "fast-follower" mentality as AI technology gets more widely adopted.

Summary

The discussion of Fabric's cutting-edge data stack architecture that delivers end-to-end AI-augmented capabilities feels like a fitting place to close out this TinyTechGuide and reflect on the insights gained throughout our journey.

Throughout this TinyTechGuide, the importance of a thoughtful selection of analytics technologies has been stressed. Rather than being swayed by the array of hyperbolic, tech-first approaches that risk overwhelming data leaders with excessive vendor and feature comparisons, the focus should be on form, function, and business needs.

This functional exploration of the Modern Data Stack will undoubtedly serve as a valuable roadmap to navigate the complexities of enterprise data stacks in the coming years.

Also, let's address the elephant in the room. The data analytics market is saturated—possibly over-saturated.

Thousands of venture capital-funded start-ups have made their way into the space, each striving to discover and exploit a niche. However, as the market temperature eventually levels off, differentiation and quality will become paramount, including pushing past the perceived safety of bundles offered only by cloud service providers.

In this market, the Modern Data Stack finds itself under increased pressure to streamline and rationalize due to the need for cost controls and the complexity of integration. A wave of consolidation and convergence in the market is likely on the horizon, with the most influential companies securing their growth and survival through their relentless focus on solving business needs.

This dynamic landscape demands that data teams (and their leaders) remain adaptable, always striving to learn and evolve alongside the tech. It is an exciting time to be part of the data analytics industry. We all should be eager to see how these trends shape the future of data stacks.

Stay curious, stay informed, and stay flexible. Remember—the value of data is only as good as the insights we draw from it!

Chapter 8 References

[1] Balik, Lauren. "How Fivetran + Dbt Actually Fail." Medium. October 13, 2022. https://medium.com/@laurengreerbalik/how-fivetran-dbt-actually-fail-3a20083b2506.

[2] Wang, Sarah, and Martin Casado. "The Cost of Cloud, a Trillion Dollar Paradox." Andreessen Horowitz. May 27, 2021. https://a16z.com/2021/05/27/cost-of-cloud-paradox-market-cap-cloud-lifecycle-scale-growth-repatriation-optimization/.

[3] Schmarzo, Bill, and Kirk Borne. *The Economics of Data, Analytics, and Digital Transformation: The Theorems, Laws, and Empowerments to Guide Your Organization's Digital Transformation*. Birmingham: Packt, 2020.

[4] Rao, Anand. "Solving AI's ROI Problem. It's Not That Easy." PwC. July 20, 2021. https://www.pwc.com/us/en/tech-effect/ai-analytics/artificial-intelligence-roi.html.

[5] Dehghani, Zhamak. "Data Mesh Principles and Logical Architecture." martinFowler.com. December 3, 2020. https://martinfowler.com/articles/data-mesh-principles.html.

[5] Venetsanopoulos, Constantinos. "The Coming Era of Data as Code." The New Stack. January 4, 2021. https://thenewstack.io/the-coming-era-of-data-as-code/.

[6] McGregor, Jim. "Generative AI Breaks the Data Center: Data Center Infrastructure and Operating Costs Projected to Increase to over $76 Billion by 2028." *Forbes*. May 12, 2023. https://www.forbes.com/sites/tiriasresearch/2023/05/12/

generative-ai-breaks-the-data-center-data-center-infrastructure-and-operating-costs-projected-to-increase-to-over-76-billion-by-2028/.

[7] "Bring Your Data into the Era of AI." Microsoft. Accessed August 28, 2023. https://www.microsoft.com/en-gb/microsoft-fabric.

[8] "Azure Data Factory." Microsoft. Accessed August 28, 2023. https://azure.microsoft.com/en-gb/products/data-factory/.

[9] "Azure Synapse Analytics." Microsoft. Accessed August 28, 2023. https://azure.microsoft.com/en-gb/products/synapse-analytics.

[10] "OneLake, the OneDrive for Data." Microsoft. May 23, 2023. https://learn.microsoft.com/en-us/fabric/onelake/onelake-overview.

[11] "Azure OpenAI Service." Microsoft. Accessed August 28, 2023. https://azure.microsoft.com/en-gb/products/cognitive-services/openai-service.

Acknowledgments

Writing a book is a journey that takes you through highs and lows, moments of doubt, and moments of pure flow. It's a dance between creativity and discipline, passion and perseverance, and no one dances alone. Well, unless you're listening to Billy Idol's "Dancing with Myself."

With that in mind, I'd love to give special thanks to my family (Kirsteen, Lottie, and Joe) for tolerating long hours of me being squirreled away in the office bashing at the keys, to my loyal whippet Fingal who patiently waited for his walks when the chapters were done, and to friends, colleagues, and coworkers (past and present) who've all given so much time and generous support in reviewing, bouncing ideas back-and-forth, and making sure that I got across the finish line.

Thanks to Laura and Jon Webb, Damian and Sandy Rowe, Alan Ponsford, and Satvere and Alan Kyte for all their support throughout the years that we've been traveling down this analytics path. Special thanks to Scott Brown, David Matyáš, Spike Van Der Schyff, Jim Schattin, and Russell Christopher for their input and unique perspectives on the Modern Data Stack and Shaan Mistry for his support and encouragement along the way.

Remember, it's not the tech that's tiny, just the book!™
Ever onward!

About the Author

Nick Jewell, PhD, is an experienced technology evangelist with a strong financial services background who's worked across product management, product marketing, and customer success in recent years. He has shared platform roadmaps, thought leadership content, and built go-to-market experiences for prospects, customers, industry analysts, and the broader analytics community.

Deeply passionate about data literacy and analytics upskilling, Nick cofounded datacurious.ai to deliver scalable, affordable analytics learning paths to a global audience.

Nick also holds a PhD in Information Science from the University of Sheffield, was recognized as one of Corinium's Top 50 Innovators in Data and Analytics in 2019, and was featured in DataIQ's Top 100 "Most Influential in Data" lists on three separate occasions.

Follow Nick on Twitter (@NickJewell) and connect with him on LinkedIn (https://www.linkedin.com/in/nickjewell/).

Index

A

AIOps, 21

Airbnb, 17, 101

Aizenberg, Igor, 73

Alation, 138, 144

Alteryx, 86, 96, 97, 98, 99, 103, 117

Amazon DynamoDB, 44

Amazon Elastic Compute Cloud (EC2), 16, 44

Amazon Elastic MapReduce (EMR), 62, 63

Amazon Kinesis, 43, 44, 47, 76

Amazon Redshift, 17, 21, 38, 52

Amazon Simple Storage Service (Amazon S3), 18, 34, 58

Amazon Web Services (AWS), 43, 44, 62, 127, 154

AMPLab, 17, 60

analytic application frameworks, 106

annual recurring revenue (ARR), 100

anomaly detection, 30, 79, 142

Apache Airflow, 17, 99, 152

Apache Flink, 79, 80

Apache Hudi, 69

Apache Iceberg, 69

Apache Kafka, 42, 76

Apache Samza, 79

Apache Spark, 17, 59, 60, 61, 62, 67, 68, 69, 81

Apache Storm, 79

application monitoring, 29

application programming interface (API), 30, 34, 43, 61, 97, 110, 114, 122, 127

approximate nearest neighbor (ANN), 129

ARR, 101

Arrow, 59, 71

artificial intelligence (AI), 1

automation, 1, 20, 21, 25, 45, 72, 99, 100, 138, 142, 159

Avro, 43, 59

AWS Aurora, 153

AWS Lambda, 44, 128

AWS Sagemaker, 117

AWS SageMaker's Ground Truth, 119

Azure Data Factory, 157, 161

Azure Data Lake Storage, 18

Azure OpenAI Service, 157, 161

B

Balik, Lauren, 148

Bard, 153

batch schedules, 35

batch windows, 35

www.ingramcontent.com/pod-product-compliance
Lightning Source LLC
Chambersburg PA
CBHW061601220326
41597CB00053B/1936